SPEAK FOR LEADERSHIP

How to Engage, Persuade,
and Inspire *Any* Audience

ALSO BY GARY GENARD

How to Give a Speech

Fearless Speaking:
Beat Your Anxiety, Build Your Confidence, Change Your Life

The Online Meetings Handbook

Gary Genard

SPEAK FOR LEADERSHIP

How to Engage, Persuade,
and Inspire *Any* Audience

Cedar &
Maitland
Press

The Genard Method
93 Concord Avenue, Suite 3
Belmont, MA 02478
www.genardmethod.com
info@genardmethod.com
(617) 993-3410

First Edition

Interior design and typesetting: Alan Barnett

ISBN: 978-1-7365556-0-6

Library of Congress Control Number: 2021918045

Printed in the United States of America

To order this book, please call (617) 993-3410,
or contact info@genardmethod.com.
Group and academic discounts are available.

Visit our website at www.genardmethod.com

Dedicated to Mrs. Merchant, who believed in me,
and who, fifteen years after fourth grade
when I ran into her at the post office,
said she recognized who I was from my eyes,
which gives a good idea of the kind of teacher she was.

TABLE OF CONTENTS

All the World's a Stage

All the world's a stage,
And all the men and women merely players;
They have their exits and their entrances,
And one man in his time plays many parts.

—*William Shakespeare,* As You Like It

Let's talk about the face you show the world.

This is a book on speaking as a leader to influence audiences. In it, I share insights from a lifetime of performing, lecturing, coaching, and training to show how you can speak at your very best. Why does that need to happen when you speak in public? Because whatever level you're at in your profession—when you present, you're the leader in the room.

Leaders speak…and speakers lead.

But discussing 'public speaking' or 'presentations' doesn't tell the whole story at all. Every time you interact with others, you reveal who you are. You may simply be having a conversation. You might be contributing something at a meeting. These days it's as likely to happen in a phone call or video conference. Whether it's pitching your products or ideas, detailing your consulting services, revealing a diagnosis to a patient, or discussing strategy with a client, you influence people in your daily interactions in ways that aren't formal presentations at all. And people perceive you, and yes, judge you, according to what they hear and see.

The truth is, you're *always* giving a performance. When it comes to public speaking, you can have a lasting influence on a large audience, an individual, or groups in between. Whether it's a formal presentation, a conversation, or a chat, the way you carry yourself and express your ideas as you relate to others is vital to the influence you achieve.

So, what's the face you show your world?

And anyway, how important is all of this to you professionally? Well, it's very important. When you make your case with passion and power, your standing and career advancement may suddenly soar. Your visibility is elevated. You might even become known as a memorable speaker. Can you think of another occasion that will bring you such prominence so quickly? Public speaking makes a *big* difference—as much in today's digital world as in previous times. The histories of entire nations, in fact, have been changed by a single powerful speech.

This book is about what you can accomplish when you demonstrate leadership presence as a speaker. Chris Anderson, head of TED, said: "A successful talk is a little miracle—people see the world differently afterward."[1] And as Shakespeare reminded us, performance is so central to human existence that it is an inescapable part of our lives: He said, "All the world's a stage, and all the men and women merely players."

If *all the world* is a stage, that means you're actually performing in ordinary conversations as well as in speeches and presentations. I'll have more to say in these pages about how you can command a room in all of those other situations—interpersonal communication, pitches, meetings, and other everyday scenarios as well as speeches that place you in the spotlight.

When it comes to speaking to be heard, the more you can appeal to listeners through your stage presence, the more successful a communicator you'll be. You'll also become more confident and comfortable.

Speak for Leadership is a primer on influencing others and getting the results you want every time you speak, but especially in public speaking. Look up the term "presence," the quality you need to truly succeed when speaking for leadership. You'll find that no one definition does the term justice. How could they, when achieving presence in performance includes public speaking, theater, music, dance, singing, sports, and other endeavors? This book examines the concept in terms of successfully speaking to others to improve their lives. Just as important, it explains all of the elements you need to achieve presence in this exciting realm of performance.

Why do I know about any of this? I've spent every decade of my life—including the first one—in some kind of live performance, as a singer, musician, actor, professor of communications, keynote speaker, and speech coach to groups and individuals worldwide. My company, The Genard Method, is dedicated to inspiring people from all walks of life to discover the power of their own voice and to reach their full potential as communicators. That is what I offer you in this book. And here's something that should entice you. Together, we'll explore how to command a stage and succeed with listeners through a *theater-based system of public speaking performance.*

Why theater as a model? For over two thousand years, drama has provided the world's most powerful tools for inspiring and energizing audiences. Theater-based techniques can help you make people care while they trust in your honesty and credibility. When you take command of a speech or presentation or speak powerfully at a meeting, what you say is far more likely to stick. If you use the tools that I'll be giving you, you'll be personally memorable as well. Speak as a leader and you'll "help make people want what you want them to want."[2] Equally important, you'll spur stakeholders to take the actions you want them to take, in a way that benefits them. Again: whatever your job title, every time you speak, you are the leader in the room.

So, welcome to the theater of your own life. After all, if you think of your life as a movie, who else can play the leading character as well as you? Talk about the role of a lifetime!

Get ready to influence people—whether it's a single individual or a conference audience—at an entirely new level. Take a breath and prepare to become a more confident, charismatic, and successful communicator. The skills you will learn in these pages are not extraordinary. In fact, I want you to be the best *you* can possibly be, with the talents, passion, and ambition you possess at this very moment.

Always remember that for an audience—internal or external, local or global—what they see is what they get. The 'what' here, is you. And to those people, the you performing in this moment is literally who you are.

CHAPTER 1

Can You Learn Leadership Presence?...*YES!*

> Be here now.
>
> —*Ram Dass*

> There is no good singing, there is
> only present and absent.
>
> —*Jeff Buckley*

Mastering the art of speaking to others is the most important skill you can acquire as a professional. It's always been that way—from ancient times to today's virtual environments. Exciting things can happen when you as speaker take the stage.

But such magic isn't limited to influencing public speaking audiences. Certainly, if you're an executive, entrepreneur, motivational speaker, CEO, or anyone who speaks at meetings, this book provides powerful techniques for reaching and moving listeners. And, if you're a musician, dancer, singer, or other in-person performer, it will show you a transformative approach for going about your craft.

That's because *Speak for Leadership* is all about performing at your best. And if there's one thing you need to understand to touch people's lives, it's that you have the power to do so through how you speak to and influence them. As I said in the introduction, you're always performing when you deal with others. This book will show you how to bring your best self "on stage" when it comes to sharing the things that you're passionate about.

Therefore, our first important lesson is as follows: you can *learn* the presence that will allow you to do this.

Because I'm an actor and speech coach, I'll be focusing on how you can accomplish this level of presence on the public speaking stage: 'stage presence.' The focus, however, will not be on getting listeners turned on to the material of your speech or presentation, necessary as that is. Other books, including my earlier book *How to Give a Speech*, deal with that desirable outcome. This book is about getting audiences passionate about *you* as a performer in a way that leads directly to influence.

And why wouldn't audiences feel that way? Whatever business or professional information you discuss when you speak, you are absolutely unique. You're literally the only person in the world who can say what you need to say, the way you're able to say it.

Listeners don't separate the message and the messenger. If they like you, they will be much more open to what you're saying or showing them. Equally exciting: performance is the most powerful medium through which to reach people about anything. It's the reason people like me go into acting. Ultimately, it's also the reason why you are willing to speak to groups of total strangers if it means getting your message out.

You make it all come alive in a way that's simply not possible otherwise.

That's the idea of performance. It doesn't matter whether it's live, part of a video conference, or even on a recorded webinar. In every one of those cases, it's you, speaking in the moment when you are heard or recorded, conveying the importance and immediacy of your topic. To the extent that audience members get why any of it matters, it's you that's making that happen.

That's the reason you need as much leadership presence as you can muster.

But here's the really good news: you can learn to be fully present and exciting when you speak, even if you think—especially if you think—that it involves some kind of aura you just don't possess. Speaking with presence in order to lead is a skill like any other; and this book will help you understand and develop that ability.

Are you ready to take that journey?

WHAT IS SPEAKING PRESENCE?

One of the challenges of public speaking has always been that "the rules" of effective performance tend to be too constrictive and custom-bound. In the U.S., we've gone from grand nineteenth-century oratory, to the currently fashionable talks we see online. If TED Talks are all you watch, for instance, you may think that the only way to give a good speech is to stand inside a red circle and talk for 18 minutes.

But true artists break rules...and the best ones *make* the rules. Although, we can't all be artists or groundbreakers, our personal goal should never be to speak to a formula. We can have this outlook even while understanding that conferences, panels, and other events have carefully thought-out schedules and time slots for speakers that we must follow.

Where's the balance? The truth is the exceptional speaker creates something unique and valuable within the dictates of the medium, like a poet in a sonnet or haiku. Connecting with one's audience and bringing about positive change is what matters, whatever the venue or specific information in your speech.

Well, then, how do you achieve that connection? At this point, we really need to know what we mean by "presence," even if it's not a hard-and-fast definition. This phrase is extremely hard to define.

So, how do we gain a sense of the special and transformative nature of stage presence in speaking for leadership? We can talk about the "passion, confidence, and comfortable enthusiasm"[1] we recognize in those who display it. A contributor to *Dance Magazine* said this about it: "It's the something that draws your eye to the dancer—the sparkle, the shine, an energy that pulls focus, be it subtly or with a brazen demand."[2] When practiced with great skill, it can turn a performer in any medium into a kind of mesmerist who invisibly weaves a spell right in front of us.

The great eighteenth- and nineteenth century German dramatist Johann Wolfgang von Goethe made it a central concept of his "Rules for Actors" when he wrote:

> An actor standing alone on the stage should remember that he is called to fill out the stage with his presence, and this is so much the more when the attention is focused solely upon him..... The stage is to be regarded as a figureless tableau for which the actor supplies the figure.[3]

The actor "is called to fill out the stage with his presence." And the stage itself is a "figureless tableau for which the actor supplies the figure." Imagine that Goethe is discussing public speaking rather than acting. Can you think of a more powerful image of how your presence on stage allows you not only to deliver information, but also to move audiences?

The Importance of Energy. A good way to grasp this idea is to think in terms of energy. When someone with presence enters a room, the level of energy somehow feels different. People may stop what they're doing to look. They feel that something interesting just happened or is about to happen. It's as though a spotlight were shining on that person, one that follows them wherever they go.[4] (In the theater, in fact, we have a term for this type of spotlight: it's called a "follow spot.")

People with stage presence carry an absolute air of authority, but it always comes from them just being themselves. We can call this being themselves *at their* best; and so, it must become you, being yourself at your best. This concept is important to grasp. Otherwise, it can feel like too much of a hurdle to suddenly become someone who makes everyone's head turn when you walk into a room.

Your first action, then, for gaining true presence as a speaker, is to become comfortable being yourself. There's no more important bar to clear than that first one. In fact, trying to be "better" or different from who you really are will inhibit your ability to develop any real magnetism on stage. People are drawn to others who are completely themselves—totally authentic and in the moment. That's probably because many of us have trouble being those two things even when we're off stage!

This is where the world of acting can help. Did you ever wonder why we believe actors whose names we know well (Christian Bale, say, or Cate Blanchette) are really the characters they're playing? It's not due to artifice—as we might think at first—but *truth*. That's because instead of trying to give a towering performance, the experienced actor simply plays the life of the character, moment by moment as it unfolds in the script. Actors and actresses have the skill of suspending their own knowledge of what is about to happen in a scene, so they can react to it honestly and realistically. (It's called "the illusion of the first time".) Since they are totally in the moment, they can react organically to what is happening right now.

What emerges is a true emotional response by the character to that moment. What we don't see is all the character study and the invention of a life for that person offstage, discussions with the director about intentions and motivations, the exhausting rehearsals, and all the rest.

This is exactly the same kind of truth and authenticity you need for developing speaking presence! In your case, it involves conveying the truth of what you're saying to listeners. But just as with the actor, it's about that truth, not giving a great performance. This is a bedrock principle to keep in mind in speaking for leadership.

Consequently, BEING PRESENT is the first requirement for succeeding with audiences, whether you're an actor or a speaker.[5] It truly is all about connecting. That is what's behind the first of my two definitions of public speaking presence (to be accepted as absolutely not the last word on the subject):

> *The convergence of our mental, emotional, physical, and spiritual selves in a moment of spoken performance while connecting with others.*

My second definition, which I hope is equally valid, is much more down to earth:

> *A spoken performance that genuinely moves an audience without being phony.*

WHY DO YOU NEED IT?

To give a performance that's truly magical, you can't do it the way a stage magician does—by putting something over on everyone. If anything, you need to accomplish the opposite. You must show everyone who you are in terms of authenticity, while sharing something of great value: the truth, as it relates to your topic. This is in fact the task of a lifetime when it comes to influential public speaking—*your* lifetime.

As James A. Whittaker puts it in *The Storyteller's Spell book*:

> Your life and career are spent showcasing yourself, your abilities, ideas, and contributions.... Simply put, your ideas and insights mean *nothing* if they cannot be transmitted to others. Without a good story, and the ability to tell it, your skill and passion remain trapped inside you instead of impacting the wider world.

There is a huge difference Whittaker tells us, "between transmitting facts to an audience and transforming the way people think." Stage presence in fact is a life skill. [6]

It's also a form of mindfulness. If you think of it in this way, you'll realize that 'stage' presence isn't limited to being on stage at all. It's simply a form of being present in performance, and of being *in* the present. The concept of fully occupying the present moment is actually the core idea of mindfulness.

You can benefit from this form of mindfulness or presence in any aspect of your life. That certainly includes communicating with others. Of course, public speaking is the situation where you're most likely to share your ideas with the largest audiences and gain the highest profile. Developing presence when you speak, then, magnifies your ability to be present and impact listeners positively.

There's another intriguing idea here that isn't often remarked upon: that this isn't a one-way street. Both you as presenter *and* the audience are necessary to create presence. Having people around you who are fully in the moment brings YOU into the present. The back-and-forth dynamic that takes place when you speak before any audience is a unique format for achieving leadership presence!

CLOSE-UP

It's Not All About the Data!

Presenters everywhere make a fundamental mistake, however. Too often, they focus solely on the information they need to deliver, rather than the overall purpose they're trying to achieve in their speech. Speaking in public, however, is always about influencing one's audience, and never about simply delivering information. The material in your presentation is only one aspect of achieving that influence. The more vital element is you. That's because the content is always filtered through your unique knowledge of it, along with your experience and the passion you display.

If the essential data concerning the topic were all that mattered, wouldn't an email, text, or social media post accomplish the task?

A speech, on the other hand, is a form of community—and that's something infinitely more immediate and possessing much greater impact. And it only really takes place if the speaker is present and making a connection with his or her listeners.

Someone once referred to the theater as "a state of mind that both audience and actors can share and experience."[7] It's exactly the same in a speech or presentation. There's a reason that the words "present" and "presence" both have their origin in the Latin word *praesentia*.

When we think of presence like this, we arrive at an inescapable conclusion: that the skills needed to develop it aren't extraordinary in any way. They're the same ones you use to persuade, inspire, and entertain people when you talk about anything you're interested in. And the more you can establish a relationship with them, the more they will like you and want to listen. This book will show you how to use these "people skills" that you already have to their greatest effect in public speaking. That's why the answer to the question: "Can you learn leadership presence?" is a resounding YES!

HOW DO YOU ACQUIRE IT?

You're probably wondering at this point: "What are the practical skills that will allow me to be fully present and hold audiences spellbound?"

Before I can answer that, I have to pose another question: What do we mean by public speaking *performance*? As I've said, it's a form of communication that doesn't only involve speeches and presentations. What about the many other forms of speaking including conversations, networking, job interviews, pitching ideas, contributing at meetings (both live and virtually), and so on?

All of these situations call upon exactly the same skills you use in public speaking. These include vocal delivery, body language, eye contact, listening and displaying empathy, fielding questions and challenges, etc. These interactions accomplish the same purpose as speaking in public in terms of being heard and influencing people. And often, there's a public setting involved.

But something mysterious happens when we compare these situations with the formal occasions we know as "public speaking." When we're tasked with speaking formally, i.e., in a presentation or speech, we tend to focus on our limitations in ways that we don't when we're 'just' having a conversation. So, starting right now, I'd like you to accept that all of these scenarios require you to *share your ideas with others*. If chatting with someone doesn't make you doubt that you can speak for leadership, why should delivering a presentation with a slide deck or a spreadsheet make that happen?

Successful Public Speaking Means Connecting with Listeners

People who come to public speaking from an administrative or event-oriented standpoint tend to underestimate the power of performance. For instance, Chris Anderson of TED says "getting the words, story, and substance right is a much bigger determinant of success or failure than how you stand or whether you're visibly nervous."[8]

I don't believe this is true. As a Ph.D., I've attended enough academic conferences to tell you that nearly every speaker gets to center-stage and reads their research paper, word for word. The "substance" is certainly right. But the experience is about as exciting as watching an animal lie sleeping in a cage at a zoo. There's no energy and vitality—no blood racing through the veins.

No matter how technical, scientific, or analytical a talk is it has to have some of that blood in its veins. Here's an example.

I often train physicians and hospital leadership teams in presentation performance. A few years ago, I was conducting a daylong seminar for a group of oncologists. Over lunch, one of them leaned over to me and said, "You know, I travel around the world to hear leading scientists and researchers in my field. But so often, this person will get to the lectern and bury his nose in his notes and drone on and on. Within five minutes, everyone is looking at their cell phone. I get so frustrated, because this is someone who is doing truly exciting work. And it all turns out to be so un-engaging that it seems a huge waste of time."

Clearly, these scientist-speakers are getting the substance right. But the absence of performance skills is a key factor in their failure as speakers.

The lesson here seems obvious: The moment of connection between you and the audience is the very essence of successful public speaking.

Have you heard the expression, usually said of actors, "he could read the phone book and make it interesting"? In other words, the performance itself can be riveting regardless of the substance.

Here's a situation where I experienced this myself:

When I was training as an actor at the Webber Douglas Academy of Dramatic Art in London, I would see a play at least twice a week. After all, I had the entire West End (London's equivalent of Broadway), as well as The Royal National Theatre at my disposal.

One evening, some of us managed to get tickets for Harold Pinter's *No Man's Land* at the National. Starring in the play were John Gielgud and Ralph Richardson, the two actors who—along with Laurence Olivier—are often considered the greatest actors of the twentieth century. For the first twenty minutes or so of this play, there are only two characters on stage—the ones Gielgud and Richardson were portraying. I was mesmerized by the performances of these two giants of the stage. And I distinctly remember how disappointed I was when the rest of the cast made their appearance. Here was the phone-book-effect in action: Richardson and Gielgud could literally have been reading off names in a telephone directory and I think it would have been a thrilling experience![9]

Give *Your* Audience an Experience. What does this mean for you as a speaker? Like an accomplished actor, you need to give your audience something more than the mere delivery of data. You need to offer them an experience.

Anyone can read from notes or a slide deck. Speaking with presence, however, does something very different—it jolts your audience with a surge of electricity and excitement. Remember: you're taking listeners on a journey. You're their guide. If you want the experience to be memorable for them, it has to involve a lot more than having information thrown at them.

CAN YOU ACHIEVE IT?

You may be asking yourself if this level of presence and charisma is even possible for you. Perhaps you're not a motivational speaker, C-suite executive, or a leader in your organization.

First of all, you should understand that productive stage presence is not the same as charisma (a term I'll discuss in a moment). Gaining presence will simply help you engage an audience, boost your confidence, and create a more enjoyable experience for everyone—all necessary to an effective result. It's the ordinary moments of connecting with listeners, rather than any extraordinary skills displayed, that allow you to be yourself on stage. And those are exactly the moments when you'll come through at your best.

Your public persona should always be a reflection of who you really are.

ON CHARISMA

What about this question of charisma? Doesn't coming across as a magnetic speaker mean being fascinating from the moment you walk onstage? Does stage presence require any technique at all, or is it all just mystique?[10]

If you're in the mystical camp—if you accept the definition of charisma as "a divinely conferred power or talent"[11]—you won't agree with Roger Ailes, who had this to say in his book *You Are the Message*:

> 'Charisma' is a powerful but often misunderstood word. It derives from the Greek *kharisma,* meaning favor or divine gift, and its root is *kharis,* meaning grace. The dictionary defines [it] as 'a special, inspiring quality of leadership.' It's really the ability to subtly cause others to react to you as opposed to your reacting to them. People with charisma seem to be in charge of their lives. They seem to have a goal, a purpose, a direction—in fact, a mission."[12]

Aren't the attributes of being in charge of your own life, and having a goal and a purpose within your grasp? Even if you're an extraordinary person who emits a special aura in front of others, you still have the task of meeting your public speaking audience's needs.

And if you don't possess such an aura, so what? Having a goal and a purpose, and especially caring about your audience more than you care about yourself, means to embody the type of speaking that leads to charisma.

It usually happens when you stop trying to be good and focus on being honest instead.

That's what moves the needle with audiences every time.

STAGE PRESENCE AND YOUR PERSONAL BRAND

I'd like to conclude this chapter with two areas that are increasingly important in 21st-century business. The first is your personal brand; and the second is using digital media to gain a more powerful presence.

Today, when it's possible to reach thousands or even millions of people through what you say, developing presence also means boosting your personal brand. Your image among the people who see and hear you—whether it's in person, online, in videos, or through podcasts—is a key element of your personal and professional persona.

Shaping and strengthening one's brand has become an important tool of personal empowerment. If you're in charge (and when you speak in public, you're always the one in control), you need to be exceptionally good at presenting your brand to the public.[13]

In the past, your impact was limited to the people sitting in an audience, those in your industry who heard about you, and perhaps, people who saw you in the local media. But today, "a speech can have a life far beyond the twenty or thirty minutes [you] spend in delivering it."[14]

A professional speechwriter expressed that last sentiment in 2000. At this point more than two decades later, it's a truth on steroids, since the Internet means your words can last forever.

STAGE PRESENCE, THE MEDIA, AND YOU

Today, we all need to be aware of our media appearances. You may not think of yourself as someone who appears in the media—but day-by-day, it's becoming more likely. That's because 'media' doesn't only mean the national TV networks, cable news, and NPR. It has always meant your town's weekly paper as well, along with industry magazines and journals, your local radio station, and the PR department of your organization. But now it also means podcasts, videos you post on YouTube and TikTok, and increasingly, online sites of every imaginable level of sophistication that want to interview or otherwise hear from you.

Equally important: it can also mean your own podcast, video blog ("vlog"), and the audio version of your books. These days everyone has a camera in their smartphone, and video is fast becoming more of an everyday part of our professional lives. That translates into visibility, and the opportunity to reach ever more people in your business or industry. The truth is that, many thousands of people may be judging your vocal and visual presence.

Consider how media has expanded. In 1950, there were 98 commercial television stations; in 2017 (the last year for which data are available), that number was 1,761.[15] As for radio stations, in 2013 there were an incredible 15,300 including 4,728 AM stations, 6,613 commercial FM stations, and 3,989 educational/non-profit FM stations.[16]

And what about online presence—how important is that these days? The number of daily newspapers in this country has declined, from 1,748 in 1970, to 1,286 in 2016.[17] Yet unique visitors of newspaper websites have grown, from around 7.7 million per month in 2014, to about 12.2 million in 2018.[18]

According to the PEW Research Center, the gap between the numbers of Americans who get their news via television versus online is narrowing significantly. In just one year from 2016 to 2017, the TV-versus-online news gap decreased from a 57–38 split respectively, to 50–43, or a change from a 19-point gap to just 7 points.[19] That is, almost as many people are now getting their news from the Internet as receive it from the major television news programs.

You may not like seeing yourself on video as many of my clients don't. Yet as the use of video to reach and influence others grows, your ability to be comfortable and natural on the small screen will matter more and more.

Therefore, you need to ask yourself, "Am I someone an audience would want to watch in a video clip?"

In video just as with in-person speaking, confidence sells. And engagement is the name of the game. So, the recipe for developing presence in media appearances is the same one we've been discussing: develop a listener-centered approach which is highly focused on communicating, rather than rattling on as a subject matter expert. The content of your talk will still be intact. And you won't lose any of your expertise. You'll have just made your material as well as yourself more accessible to your audience. If you perform that role well, failure will be almost impossible.

Did you ever imagine that acquiring leadership presence, as a speaker would involve simply tapping into who you are?

CLOSE-UP

The Worst Public Speaking Advice (and How to Do Better)

They say the road to hell is paved with good intentions...and I'd add, bad public speaking advice! Here are six common speech tips you may have heard, all of which are guaranteed to send you toward the nether regions of public speaking mediocrity.

1. **Presentation 'Rules'.** Nothing kills spontaneity and flexibility like presentation 'Rules.' You know them: the rule about how many slides you should show; the one about how many bullet-points a slide should contain (and the maximum number of allowable words in each one)...even how much time you should spend on each main point! Who knows where these dictates come from? If you're a budding anesthesiologist, follow them explicitly. Otherwise, place your focus on how you can reach listeners and keep them engaged on the journey you're taking together. None of you will reach the destination via a prescription.

2. **Picture your audience naked.** Surprised this one is still around? Yes, it's silly advice—but it hints at something that's even more limiting. That is, denying what's actually happening. Speeches become exciting when they reach people's hearts and minds, *right here and now.* That can never happen if you remove reality from the equation. There's no need to imagine anything about your audience, in fact. They're right in front of you, they are paying attention, and they're waiting to be influenced by you. That's the naked truth!

3. **Admit to the audience that you're nervous.** We all want listeners to believe in us. So why make it more difficult for them to do so? Admitting to the audience that you're a bundle of nerves won't inspire confidence in you. I once heard a prosecuting attorney confess to a jury in her opening statement, *"I've never done this before."* Remember, most nervousness isn't visible. Therefore, you shouldn't say you suffer from it. If you do, everyone will be watching for signs of nerves from then on, rather than listening to what you're saying! Just talk about what matters. The more you connect with your audience, the less nervous you'll feel.

4. **Always start out with a joke.** A priest, a rabbi, and a rooster walk into a bar, see? The rooster says to the bartender, "What's the difference between a joke and humor?" The bartender thinks about it a minute. Then he says, "Well, a joke is a zero-sum game that either succeeds or falls flat, so you and the entire audience are embarrassed. Humor is much safer because it's gentler, and a lot easier to relate to your topic."… That's no joke. Think of it this way: The joke you're considering using wasn't created for your talk, so you'll just be grafting it on. If you want to relax the audience, look for something connected with the topic that's humorous. Believe me it's there. Just find it!

5. **Avoid getting emotional.** Here's some news from neuroscience: data that's linked to an emotional response in a listener's brain is more strongly retained. And also, this: *all decision-making has an emotional component.* Put these two facts together and you realize that if you're looking for buy-in to your ideas, include emotion in what you're saying. Just be sure to make the emotional connection one that makes sense for these listeners, that touches their experience in some way. Being "businesslike," i.e., remaining unemotional about everything is an awful choice. Audiences want and need emotional input. It can only make your talk stronger.

6. **Calm down!** You've heard this advice concerning speaking nerves: "Calm down and you'll be fine." Not only is this basically impossible, but it can be counterproductive to an energized performance. Your speech needs the energy-rush you're getting from

adrenaline—which provides you with exactly the same physical activation whether the stimulus is pleasurable or stressful. What matters is how you *interpret* your physical response. Rather than trying to go into guru-mode (which you can't do anyway), think about how excited you are to share this information with your audience. As you've always heard, the trick is how you play the cards you're given!

CHAPTER 2

Why You're a Natural Performer

On the stage he was natural, simple, affecting;
'Twas only that when he was off he was acting.
—*Oliver Goldsmith, describing David Garrick*

You can get what you want by being who you are.
—*Roger Ailes*

Did you know that every time you speak to others, you're giving a performance? And that the times when you're getting through most effectively may be the moments when you're not trying to perform at all?

Performance is such an essential part of our social lives, in fact, that we don't recognize either the need to do it or our consummate skills in accomplishing it well. Much more so than the other primates, *we are natural performers.* But when it comes to speaking in public, for some reason we insist on telling ourselves we're no good at it.

That's a mindset that inhibits both our comfort level and effectiveness.

When we underrate our own communication abilities, it keeps us from connecting effortlessly with audiences. We shy away from the invitation because we feel the task is beyond our abilities. Pitches, conference speeches, proposals to the leadership team, or speaking at all-hands-on-deck meetings are formal and intimidating situations. We consider them to be out-of-the-ordinary moments requiring exceptional skills, and wonder how we can ever rise above our quite ordinary competencies to perform them well.

But as sociologist Erving Goffman pointed out in his book, *The Presentation of Self in Everyday Life*, we are always performing. Because of the intensely social nature of our lives, we adjust our demeanor and actions—every day and in every situation—to fit in with the people and circumstance of the moment. The 'you' at your company's Monday morning meeting, for instance, is different from the 'you' at home that same evening with your family. And that particular 'you' isn't the same as the one who is attending your 20th high school reunion…or, for that matter, the one trying to talk your way out of that speeding ticket.

Do you know the saying, "When in Rome, do as the Romans do"? That is exactly what we do when we adapt our behavior to the needs of the moment. And we do it easily and effortlessly, because we understand that it's an essential part of being human.

So why do we feel that when it's time to deliver a high-profile presentation, we have to become something better than our everyday selves? The attempt to do that is guaranteed to keep you from looking, sounding, moving, or feeling like yourself! All the natural spontaneity and rhythms of who you are instead get ironed out into a flat and rather uninteresting performance. After all, you're speaking for business now…and we all know that means you have to be serious, even somber.

If that also means not showing listeners who you are and why you care about them, well, *c'est la guerre.*

But you'll never succeed—in life *or* public speaking—by displaying a carefully constructed version of yourself. The alternative is much more powerful. And actually, it's a lot easier, since it's simply performing your own life.

How Are You Performing Your Life?

Part of the reason this is such an important concept is that people can only react to the performance you're giving. That's true whether you're delivering a speech or chatting with a neighbor at the supermarket. People gain impressions of who you are not by conjuring those perceptions out of thin air, but because *you've given them something to perceive.* Audiences and other listeners can't read your mind to know how you really feel about what you're saying. The performance you broadcast—in terms of voice, body language, facial expressions, eye contact, pauses, emphasis, the rhythm and urgency of your speech, along with other aspects of performance—is the one they will receive!

Audience (or listener) perceptions aren't casual matters, either. People are deciding whether they can trust you, whether you're knowledgeable about a topic, or if they should believe what you say. They are observing how you feel about them, and sometimes, your feelings toward yourself. If it's a business transaction, they are very definitely considering if they're willing to buy what you're selling, or whether they want to work with you.

The good news is in the title of this chapter, that you're a natural performer at this. You already have every tool you need to make these interactions successful, and to instill comfort and trust in those listening to you. If you want to be an effective and successful speaker, it comes down, in part, to being an honest performer.

THE THEATER OF PUBLIC SPEAKING

It's a question, then, of developing your natural talents to speak with greater comfort, confidence, and credibility. Let's call it the 'theater of public speaking.' Where will you find this place? It's the same conference room, customer's site, convention stage, or classroom where you speak now.

These everyday business locations are about to become much more exciting locales. From now on, you won't just be presenting your ideas in them—you'll be performing in a way that will steadily increase your stage presence.

To launch yourself on this journey, you first need sufficient energy.

BOOSTING YOUR PERFORMANCE ENERGY

The first step in the practical aspects of giving you greater stage presence is to make you a more *energized* speaker. Even if you already blow fuses whenever you walk into a room, this section will help you understand the relationship between energy and performance and allow you to use the combination more effectively.

The truth is you already have a natural energy that's the perfect engine for communicating with others. But public speaking requires a heightened level of performance. In public speaking as in on-stage drama, you have to be larger than life. Just the fact that you must bridge the physical space between you and listeners—and activate their thoughts and emotions when you get there—demands that you 'scale up' your performance energy.

You won't always be speaking in large venues like convention halls, of course. You might pitch your ideas in a small office, or in the proverbial elevator. Therefore, the *scale* of your presentation persona has to be right. Yet, there will always be some physical space between you and others when you speak to a group. Ultimately, it is up to you to find the balance between naturalness in terms of intimacy and the public conversation you're engaged in. Also, of course, you must factor in the demands of the space in which you are presenting. Always remember this, then: *the venue itself is an important player in the successful performance of your speech or presentation.*

However large or small your performance area is, you need to fill it appropriately: restrained gestures and movements for small spaces, more expansive ones when you're trying to reach people far away from you. If you're in a cavernous convention hall, there may be a Jumbotron to help you. But tech solutions like that are only there to take what you generate and broadcast it sufficiently; you are always the focus of what the audience sees and hears, and so your "size" has to be right.

Chapter 7 in *Speak for Leadership* treats body language and its importance in terms of space; and Chapter 11 discusses the ways that you can command a stage. For now, let's talk about why the physical dimension of your performance is important at all—and how you can use it to your best advantage.

THE PHYSICAL DIMENSION

The playhouses in the two greatest theatrical eras—the ancient Greek amphitheaters and the Elizabethan "thrust" stage—were conceived to maximize the power of the drama and the audience's response. In ancient Athens, the playing area or *orchestra* was circular; the seating area (*theatron*) rose upward from it in a way that allowed everyone to see and hear clearly what was going on in the play, no matter how far away each person was sitting. Nineteen hundred or so years later, the Elizabethan *thrust stage* of Shakespeare's time (a design still seen today in many regional theaters in the U.S.) literally juts out into the house with the audience on three sides of the actors. In both these theaters, the shape of the performance area—and the physical relationship between actor and audience that resulted from it—mattered as much as anything spoken by the players.

FIGURE 2-1. Ancient Greek Theater

FIGURE 2-2. Elizabethan-Style Thrust Stage

Now consider the modern playhouse: the typical auditorium or Broadway theater. It usually contains a huge "proscenium arch," and row after row of seats marching away from the stage. The audience's seating area, though arranged on a slight upward incline, is much flatter than in the Greek amphitheaters; and spectators are nowhere near the performers, as they were in Shakespeare's time.

In fact, it's hard to conceive of a stage-and-auditorium design that would be more limiting in terms of any intimacy between performer and theatergoer. Now consider the hotel ballroom or convention stage where many business presentations take place, with chairs arranged on a flat surface over a spacious area. These venues are even worse when it comes to connecting with one's audience. Yet it is your responsibility to do so, wherever your listeners are located in relation to you as the speaker.

Whether you present in a cavernous hall or tiny conference room, *you must own the space you speak in.* And the place where that starts is ownership of your own body. As performance coach Patsy Rodenburg reminds us, "We know long before someone speaks whether we will listen to him or her. We know as soon as an actor walks onto the stage whether he will engage us."[1]

You must, then, acquire the skill of demanding that people listen to you before you utter your first word! The initial step is this process is to know how to display confidence physically. How important is this? A recent study of presentations to raise venture capital found that the best gauge for predicting success wasn't the person's credentials or even their pitch. It was how strongly they displayed confidence, comfort, and passionate enthusiasm.[2]

How to Display Confidence Physically. That word *passion* is instructive here. To gain practical knowledge of how to use the physical dimension for speaking presence—to make it happen for you on stage—you need to understand the mind-body connection. Your emotional state is particularly relevant, as it's tied to what you're doing and showing bodily.

For some reason, we seem to understand this only in one direction. We know that the way we feel tends to express itself physically. When we're sad, for instance, we may cry; and when we're happy we smile. But it occurs in the opposite direction as well, so that *the way we hold ourselves and move elicits a specific emotional response inside us.*

You can easily test this yourself right now. Stand tall with your shoulders in place, feet slightly apart, and with your chest thrust out. Don't you feel confident and ready? Now, allow your shoulders to fall and your chest to cave inward. Bend slightly at the spine, and place your hands one palm over the other in your crotch area. This posture is virtually an advertisement for powerlessness!

Here's a way to remind yourself to display the right message physically:

HOW YOU STAND AFFECTS YOUR STANDING WITH YOUR AUDIENCE.

Your mind and body consider the physical and the emotional to be a single state. Why wouldn't this happen? Your body and your brain have a lifetime of experience interpreting each other's signals! You hold yourself, move, make facial expressions, and gesture based on what you're feeling. Acknowledging this is priceless information in understanding how you're coming across to others:

> The way you carry yourself is a source of personal power—the kind of power that is the key to presence. It's the key that allows you to unlock yourself—your abilities, your creativity, your courage, and even your generosity. It doesn't give you skills or talents you don't have; it helps you to share the ones you do have. It doesn't make you smarter or better informed; it makes you more resilient and open. It doesn't change who you are; it allows you to be who you are."[3]

Your Physicality and Stage Presence

Now consider the implications of this when it comes to an audience's response to you. If what your body is doing makes *you* feel a certain way—why wouldn't it bring about a similar response in listeners? Your physical stance, posture, gestures, and movement will *cause* an emotional response in audiences the same way it does in you.

We'll look much more closely at using physical expression later in the book. At this point, it will help to begin thinking of your physicality as part of stage presence. Practice three techniques in particular:

1. **Stand and move with confidence.** Improve your posture if you need to, and be aware of whether you're sitting straight or slouching. Develop the habit of maintaining eye contact even if you're thinking of what to say next. Some speakers find this a real challenge, as their next point seems to be written on the ceiling or the floor!

2. **Fill the stage**. That really means: don't be afraid to use all parts of your performance area. That can consist of anything from a few square feet at the end of a conference table, to the wide stage of a convention hall. Our brains are biased toward visual information, and so you need to be showing audiences something visual as well as discussing concepts with words.

3. **Boost your energy level when you start to speak**. Actually, do it *before* you speak. As soon as listeners observe that you are an energetic person, they'll assume you will help energize them.

Accomplish these three things and everyone will get a clear sense that you're present and ready for the business at hand. As, indeed, you will be.

WHY YOU'RE A PROFESSIONAL SPEAKER

Do you really need to perform at such a high level if you're routinely speaking at meetings, delivering a pitch, or walking listeners through a PowerPoint presentation? Yes, and here's why:

I mentioned the 'theater of public speaking' earlier in this chapter. Let's accept, then, that public speaking is like theater in many respects. And since theater involves actors speaking in public, it's also true that theater is public speaking. This public-speaking-and-theater connection is a reminder that our job is to give audiences something above the ordinary. Our ideas should seem fresh and immediate and unfolding right there in front of the audience—so they become what voice coach Cicely Berry called 'thoughts in action.'[4]

To flesh this out a bit, I'll share with you part of a keynote that I recently delivered to a state bar association. My topic was why everyone in the auditorium was a professional speaker. That wouldn't have been true if I meant that all of these lawyers were motivational speakers.

But that wasn't my point. I was referring to the fact that they—just like you—are 'professional speakers' in that they speak on behalf of their profession. The link, I believe, is perfectly understandable if you think of it in that way. That is, you share with the celebrity on the lecture circuit the need to be a dynamic and effective presenter. And like them, you should leave the audience better off for having heard you speak.

There's an article that I shared with my audience at the state bar meeting by Jim McElhaney, former Litigation columnist for the American Bar Association Journal that sums this up beautifully. It concerns the true story of a young attorney. This newbie lawyer had a novel theory about a product safety act. He wanted to use it in an upcoming case on behalf of his firm's client, a manufacturing company. His boss asked him to present his theory to the client's chief counsel for consideration. The young lawyer's presentation didn't go well, however. He wasn't as prepared as he needed to be, and he couldn't answer the chief counsel's tough questions very convincingly.

On the drive back to the law firm, the attorney's mentor asked what the young man had learned from the experience. Then the older man provided the answer himself: "Every time you say something as a lawyer, you are making a professional presentation."[5] What he meant was that the young lawyer was a professional speaker.

And so are you. Chances are you speak to stakeholders frequently in your job, playing the role that's expected of you in each situation. Since the topics of those discussions matter to listeners, you need the poise and confidence of a professional speaker. It's as simple as that.

The rest of this book will help you rise to that challenge.

CLOSE-UP

Performance Techniques: Setting the Stage for Success

Whenever you speak in public, it's a performance. Consequently, you'd better know how to engage and activate audiences. From conversations to keynotes, you need to fully access your passion, presence, and professionalism to serve your listeners.

Performance-based techniques will help you tap into your most powerful instrument for succeeding as a speaker—yourself. Actors' tools like the ones below are custom-made to allow your confidence, impact, and influence to soar.

Here are some vital theater-inspired techniques to get you to the next level of poise and prestige as a speaker. They will allow you to set the stage for your own success!

Stage Presence and Authenticity

This is the most important of all oral communication techniques based in the theater. In speaking powerfully, you must draw upon all of your means of expression: your physical presence, voice, gestures, storytelling, as well as compelling content. Your job is never merely to deliver information, but to *create influence* based on an important message. That requires embodying the techniques of effective performance.

Diaphragmatic Breathing

Most speakers breathe shallowly because of self-consciousness and nervousness. To project a strong presence, however (and to reach the back of a large room), diaphragmatic breathing is necessary. This type of "belly breathing" produces a full, resonant voice that has the sound of authority. It's the ideal method of breathing for persuasive and influential speaking.

Relaxation and Focus Techniques

Being a relaxed speaker is important, but you must combine relaxation with a laser-like focus on your audience and message. Actors stay loose but poised, ready to respond with power while making it all look easy. Like a cat about to spring, they know not to waste an ounce of energy. When your energy is that focused, you can think on your feet and respond effectively to what audiences are giving you, as they in turn respond to what you're saying.

Being Present in the Moment

As you now know, presence is often a misunderstood term. In dramatic performance, one of the things presence means is being "there" for one's fellow actors. Contrary to popular belief, not every performance of a play is exactly the same. By paying attention and being completely in the moment, the actor can react with full concentration. The result is a performance that's much more attuned to what others are giving you. That's exactly what's happening in terms of your public speaking audience's nonverbal reactions—and perhaps even questions that they ask.

Improvisation

Few techniques of the theater are as enjoyable as improvisation. It's a tool that can help professionals of all types—not just actors—think quickly and act appropriately. For team building and responding to questions and challenges, there's no substitute for training that includes improvisation. As a speaker, you don't know what will be coming from listeners as they respond to what you're telling them. It's important therefore to know not only how to survive but to thrive in every speaking situation you find yourself in.

Beats and Intentions

This is one of the most interesting applications of theater techniques to the world of public speaking. Actors pay close attention to the motives and intentions that drive a character's behavior. There are intentions for the entire play or movie, a single scene, and for "beats" within each scene. As a presenter, you can use this approach to keep the audience focused on *this* main point within your presentation (in effect, this "beat"). It's easier for listeners to be engaged and retain what you're saying if each part of your talk is interesting in itself, and subtly different from what follows. Understanding and using beats is a powerful tool for getting audiences to respond the way you want them to, moment by moment.

Vocal Dynamics

As a speaker, you're in the business of influencing others. It may be to get people to pay attention; to buy into your vision and leadership; or to take an action you're advocating. To accomplish these things, it's vital to learn how to use your voice—the most flexible and ultimately powerful delivery tool you own for public speaking.

You may not become the next Abraham Lincoln, Martin Luther King, Jr., or Oprah Winfrey, but you can absolutely improve your vocal skills to reach the next level of skill and impact.

Body Language

Standing and moving with authority can make the difference between a mediocre encounter with an audience and a memorable one. Powerful speakers look the part as well as sound that way. There's no way around it: good nonverbal communication is essential for successful speaking. You'll be learning more in the pages below about employing movement and space to strengthen your presence and influence.

Role-Playing and Simulations

Whether the speaking situation is a high-stakes presentation, interview, sales pitch, client meeting, media appearance, or crisis, role-playing and simulations are valuable tools to train for successful outcomes. As a theater-based training system, *Speak for Leadership* will help you understand how to use role-playing scenarios to bring your practice sessions as close as possible to the real thing.

Storytelling

Delivering information can be static and boring; but telling stories makes you interesting. To connect with listeners and get them to pay rapt attention, tell a story. Stories are filled with drama and they're all about people, which is why everyone loves them. You'll be a different speaker when you find your true voice through stories so that you connect powerfully with your material. Storytelling is also an essential technique for letting everyone know you're committed enough to have prepared great stories.

Using Powerful Language

The greatest writer who ever lived was a playwright, and there's no one like Shakespeare for demonstrating the power of language. You don't need to start memorizing Shakespearean soliloquies. But by discovering how the power of language works in reaching people, you will give your presentations more color and impact. It's one of the ways your topic can come to vivid life when the "curtain" goes up. Chapters 3 and 10 share more on this topic.

PUBLIC SPEAKING AS A TRANSFORMATIVE EVENT

Now let's discuss how presence in public speaking can go much further than simply an interesting performance. Developing genuine presence isn't just a question of acquiring new skills (such as those discussed above). It's also a process of true growth, and one that involves a practical transformation.[6]

One of the ways this transformation occurs is to take you as a subject matter expert and make you into something totally different: a radically good speaker. 'Radical' because it involves a change in your mindset, one that alters your entire approach to speaking.

You can of course be an expert and not come across as an engaging presenter. In fact, that's a daily occurrence everywhere in the world. We might say it's a mistake that many otherwise brilliant people make.

When anyone asks me whom I consider to be the best public speakers, I usually say that it depends upon what they're looking for. Indeed, 'best' is a relative term with many variables that can be part of the mix. For example, if you're looking for openness, honesty, and vulnerability, Facebook executive Sheryl Sandberg is an outstanding example. You'll find a similarly easy style combined this time with the skill of connecting with the audience, in health psychologist Kelly McGonigal. If you're looking for clarity combined with a dynamic style, ServiceNow's CEO (and formerly in that role at SAP) Bill McDermott might be your speaker. And if it's a presenter who can achieve a quiet authoritative presence combined with considerable expertise, you might choose New York's Public Theater Artistic Director Oskar Eustis and his TED talk, "Why Theater Is Essential to Democracy."

But aren't *all* leaders good speakers? Actually no—and not by a long shot. There are many flavors of public speakers, and a delicious selection exists in terms of who qualifies as the best in any dimension. And let's face it, even the speakers I've named above are my choices, and your opinion may be quite different.

Being an effective leader is not necessarily equated with powerful presentation skills. On any day you'll find successful professionals who aren't effective—or even interesting—at the lectern. Public speaking is an art; and it's a very different one from running a company or organization. And if it doesn't actually require an entirely new skill set, it does involve closely understanding the task at hand and using social skills to greatest effect.

Ignoring doing so can have serious consequences as to how you're viewed in your profession, something that's all-important to a leader. Recall my story in the last chapter about the physician who attended medical conferences all over the world, only to be disappointed at the speaking skills of otherwise brilliant researchers. Such speakers have neglected any performer's main task: that of connecting with the audience. Like all staged events public speaking is a form of community, one that's all about what's happening in the moment. And the key to doing it well is pulling off a magic trick, by transforming the ability to speak to many into appearing to speak to *one*. That is what it should feel like to each audience member. Your job is to reduce the psychological distance between you and listeners, not demonstrate that you're more comfortable with your expertise and content than you are with them. Ultimately, it's the difference between a leader speaking, and speaking for leadership.

CLOSE-UP

'The Magic If'—A Formula for Transforming Your Performance

Did you know that you're as much a performer as an actor when you deliver a talk? Actors of course are wizards at making the spoken word come alive. But when you deliver a speech, you too are using a magical combination of language, voice, and physical expression to construct a different reality. Here is a fast and reliable way to speed-dial such a connection with listeners whatever your topic.

It comes from the great Russian acting teacher Constantin Stanislavski (1863–1938). Stanislavski created an acting approach based on believable emotions and physical actions that elicit those emotions. (Consider my discussion above of how using body language can help create an emotional response.)

One of Stanislavski's best-known concepts is "the Magic If". The actor asks in the early stages of rehearsal: "What would I do *if I were this character in this circumstance?*" By answering that question, the actor gets much closer to what the playwright intended than any response from his or her own life.

It's just as important that you understand the needs and motives of your audience! So why not use the 'Magic If'? Ask yourself: *"What if I were a member of this audience?—What would I be hoping to get from this talk or remarks? And what could the speaker say that would relate to me and aid my understanding?"*

Imagine how much more effective you can be if you carefully consider everything you say in terms of meeting listeners' needs. It will create more intimacy with your audience, and even better, allow you to *move* them.

WHY YOU HAVE EVERYTHING YOU NEED

If you're thinking that you don't know how to make that leap—from speaking on a topic to having an intimate conversation with an audience—please understand that it's not a leap at all. If you've been focused only on trying to be good, you've actually been avoiding getting close to listeners. And of course, you've been putting way too much pressure on yourself.

The alternative is much easier. Simply focus on serving your audience's needs, and trying to make them understand what you're saying. And please don't worry about being too vulnerable. As understandable as that may be, it's really a defense mechanism that does nothing for your credibility. When you appear before an audience whether it's live or virtual, you *are* vulnerable. Far from reacting negatively if they see that you're human, the audience will understand and accept it!

I'll have more to say on vulnerability in Chapter 10 where I discuss the essential leadership qualities. What's important here, is that the skills necessary for powerful speaking aren't extraordinary. They're *ordinary* skills, and you already possess them in abundance.

Truly, you have everything you need to develop significant stage presence. I have many clients, for instance, who are exciting speakers even though they stuttered as children. They found a way to focus not on a problem that was limiting them, but on the speaker-audience relationship and how they could tap into it. They were, in fact, eager to do so. Therefore, they worked over time to eliminate the obstacle that was holding them back.

These people understood that their job was to get their message through to people so they too could feel strongly about it. For them and for us too, it's not so much the subject matter as it is the *conversation* we're having with the audience about it. Let's get you on that wavelength.

MAKING IDEAS COME TO LIFE

You have the opportunity then to give life to dead material when you speak. In fact, that's your job and your power as a speaker. You absolutely must find it in yourself to make this happen! Your data—and even the interesting stories you tell—have been compiled, arranged, and pasted into your notes or PowerPoint deck. They've been cut and dried and preserved like a butterfly between two panes of glass.

When *you* tell that story, though, we should listen. Think of it as the difference between that butterfly on a museum wall, and flitting from flower to flower in a field as you watch. The in-person quality of your talk and your distinctive way of delivering it gives it size and immediacy. Best of all, it possesses the human dimension. Your topic will live in the minds and hearts of your listeners when you bring it to life in your voice and body. Just as the audience is the reason for your speech, you are the reason for the audience.

The Rev. Jana Childers in her book, *Performing the Word* shares this amazing thought, "Once the sermon has become ink, it can be difficult to turn it back into blood."[7] Performing the word, indeed. And how true it is that your job is to turn your own ideas and data 'back into blood' if you want your speech to have a beating heart!

Obviously, you need performance skills to make this happen. The key to reaching people successfully is not what you think you're conveying—it's what the audience understands from what you show them and what they hear in your voice, i.e., through your nonverbal communication.

You not only bring the speech to completion by speaking it.[8] You actually don't know your text *until* you speak it, the same way you don't understand your body as a communication tool until you begin to use it.

HOW TO PREPARE A SPEECH WITH YOUR AUDIENCE IN MIND

There's another way you can make ideas come to life, one that's just as important as platform skills. Your performance actually begins the moment you start thinking about your speech, long before you begin practicing it. And this is where I suggest you take an entirely new approach to speech preparation.

Most presenters use a process that I label this way:

Think ⟶ Write ⟶ Speak

You probably use this method yourself. It works like this: you have some ideas (THINK), which you then write down as notes or in a slide deck (WRITE). After editing and polishing your document, your talk is where you want it to be. If you have enough time once you have your content in place, you might get up on your feet and practice (SPEAK). If time is tight, you may skip this step.

In either case, *you will find yourself on stage delivering your speech without the correct preparation for being there.* That's because the literary document you've prepared so carefully is of little use to you once you're in what I call the *oral arena.* The task you're now faced with is establishing rapport with the audience in the here and now. And the only tool you have to accomplish it is, basically, a term paper.

Consider instead if you had built your presentation *from the first moment* as a conversation with listeners—one designed specifically to get through to them.

Think about the difference. The reason so many speakers lack presence is that they're basically reading to the audience. Their focus is on speaking aloud the words on a page or slide, instead of discussing ideas with listeners in terms they can understand.

So why not put yourself in the oral arena as early as possible? Why not get yourself ready by *conceiving and practicing a speech that was custom-made for these listeners from the start*?

You can do so by the method I've created, which I call:

Think ⟶ Speak ⟶ Write

Note the difference in the order of the three steps. Here, you think about your talk just like before. But this time, you immediately speak out loud what you're thinking of saying.

As you listen to yourself, certain key questions will be occurring to you: How do the words, phrases, and ideas sound? Is the tone right? Does the level of simplicity or sophistication fit this audience? Do you sound respectful, upbeat, and inspirational? Will what you're saying resonate with the audience's needs and desires? And in more practical terms: are the points you're making clear and concise with smooth transitions between the segments?

By using this method, you will discover that at times a word, phrase, or remark *won't* sound right, for any number of reasons. You'll then have to think about making that point in another way. By working in this manner, you'll be placing yourself in the audience's seats ahead of time, and helping your upcoming listeners to understand.

As soon as what you're saying comes out the way you want it to sound—and always in terms of the audience's understanding—write it down. By the time you're finished, you'll be halfway down the road of having a speech that resonates with these listeners. You'll also have put in a highly productive practice session.

The result is that you'll save yourself time and maybe, some embarrassment. You won't instead find out at the moment of performance that your literary gem doesn't actually work as a speech.

WHY YOU ARE THE MESSAGE

If you only work from notes or a manuscript without exploring your text through your voice and body, you'll be depriving your audience of the *actual life* of your performance. It would be like offering them a photograph instead of a taste of a sumptuous dessert.

It is only through you that the emotional authenticity of your ideas emerges. Do you think this happens if you just read notes or PowerPoint slides? The text is liberated by you. Just as in the theater, a story is made flesh by you on stage.[9] You unleash its life and its power, making it accessible to the audience.[10] As Ailes reminds us, *you are the message:*

> You can't just assume the audience is interested only in the words you've written down. If that were the case, you could save yourself a lot of trouble by staying home and just mailing them your speech. Then they could read it on Saturday, when they have more time to concentrate on it. First and foremost, the audience is interested in you, and that means you've got to put something of yourself on the table.[11]

The Audience Is Interested In You

For the audience, you should be as interesting as anything you're saying. And since you're a natural performer (as we saw at the beginning of this chapter), you don't have to try to *do* anything to be authentically interesting.

Exactly like an actor, you should believe in what you're saying at all times and completely. If you don't believe, why are you up there? If you tailor your performances so there are no visible "seems," it will be as real for listeners as it is for you.

That's because when you believe wholeheartedly in what you're saying, you express yourself naturally and openly. Vocal choices, gestures, facial expressions, and your enthusiasm all announce themselves in terms of your topic. When you enjoy what you're doing, you control the rhythm and relate easily to listeners. Isn't all of this beginning to sound like stage presence?

Perhaps the best outcome is that we will accept the truth of your performance. Just as acting is not about the actor,[12] a speech is not about you. It's about the truth of what you're saying *filtered through and expressed by you.*

The more you accept the paradox that to give a good performance you can't try to do so, the more you'll be serving the truth of what you're saying. Commit yourself to sharing that in terms of your audience's needs, and you can become an extraordinary speaker.

CHAPTER 3

How to Make
Yourself Memorable

I returned, and saw under the sun, that the race is not to the swift,
nor the battle to the strong, neither yet bread to the wise, nor yet
riches to men of understanding, nor yet favour to men of skill;
but time and chance happeneth to them all.

—Ecclesiastes, 9:11

The moment you stop trying to be a memorable public speaker is the
moment you're able to become one. Don't think of the magnitude of
your performance, though you can consider the importance of the
speech. Like the actor performing Shakespeare or Chekhov or the musician playing Mozart, the merit of the material and how it can affect listeners is what you are there to serve.

As with all things that approach greatness, you can't get there by
thinking small. 'Small' here means focusing on your own performance;
while to be great, you need to think of the big ideas and the people whose
lives you're changing. After all, you have no control of anyone's opinion
of you. But if you try to understand and convey the truth of your speech,
you can do your best and let it go at that. If you've done your job and are
there to share something that really matters to your audience, they will
listen, appreciate your effort—and perhaps even act upon it. This is the
path you take to becoming a memorable public speaker.

Still, there are ways you can help the process along. That's what this
chapter is all about.

You don't need exceptional abilities to be a memorable speaker. You *do* need a total level of commitment, however. Everyday people become extraordinary persuaders when they are a hundred percent committed to what they are saying. Consider Candy Lightner, the founder of Mothers Against Drunk Driving or MADD. After her thirteen-year-old daughter, Cari was killed by a drunk driver in 1980, Candy founded an organization that within six years included 600,000 members in forty-seven states. An ordinary citizen, Lightner became a powerful advocate for stronger drunken driving laws. She testified before state and federal legislatures, deploying her fierce commitment to save lives.[1]

Your passion for your topic—and the urgency to get it across to others—is the equal of any sophisticated speaking technique. The deeper your belief, the more persuasive you will be.

That's because of the level of engagement between performer and audience, and especially the fact that it happens in real time. As in theater, a speech or presentation isn't a one-way street.[2] The audience is always an active participant in whatever is happening on stage. This level of engagement is what feeds the performer, inviting him or her to become even more committed to making a connection with listeners. Spectators can "catch emotions" from actors. Since all of this is experienced by everyone in the same place and at the same time, it has much more in common with a face-to-face conversation than watching a film, TV program, or surfing online.[3]

WHAT DO YOU WANT TO SHARE?

So, what do you want to share to make all of this happen? Can you put your finger on what will engage, interest, and even excite an audience?

Isn't that supposed to be the whole reason why you're speaking? Naturally, this means focusing on listeners' needs rather than your own. To get yourself on the right wavelength, make the audience the center of your universe in your own mind. (See my "Six Rules of Effective Public Speaking" on page 44.)

Know Your Purpose and Why Your Topic Matters to Listeners

You should really be asking yourself , "What can I say that will be of benefit to these listeners?" To get audiences moved and then activated, they must understand why your topic matters to their lives. But before you can share that message with them, you have to establish your true purpose in your own mind. Since a speech's purpose always has to do with benefitting listeners, clearly knowing that purpose is the key to getting the audience to relate to that topic. That means letting them know early on in your talk what *their* connection to the subject is.

Recently, I was working along these lines with a client. This human resource professional had a compelling story to tell—in truth, it was literally a life-and-death situation, as someone had died in the course of what happened that day. Her willingness to describe this event was meant to move and impart a vital lesson to listeners. Yet for four-fifths of the story, her talk wasn't particularly engaging or even interesting.

How could that be? It seemed to me my client wasn't clear on the purpose of her talk. She recognized the power of the story. She just wasn't telling it in a way that made it clear from the beginning what it had to do with the lives of the people listening to her.

She began by reciting in detail her workday leading up to the shocking incident. That part of the story was not only dry and mundane, but it also clearly centered on her. I could imagine the listeners saying, "What does this have to do with me?"

At that point in our practice session, I asked her why she intended to give this speech. What would it accomplish in the minds and hearts of listeners—what did she want it to achieve? Most important: *How did she want people to think, feel, and act once they had heard this story?*

Her answer was that she wanted them to appreciate all those small moments in an average day, because those moments equaled their life. She wanted people to appreciate—just as she had the day the person had died—how precious and fleeting such moments were. When she told me that, I said, "Wonderful. Now let's show the audience the reason you're sharing this true story with them."

And that's the way it works: Give your listeners a roadmap—not only where you and they are about to go together, but *why* you're leading them there.

It might sound something like this: "I'd like to share an experience I had recently, because I think it's something you can all relate to." Or this: "I want to talk about something that I think matters to all of us here at the company." Then explain briefly why whatever you've just said is true. You'll discuss it in detail in a moment. But what you're saying now is: "Here is why you should pay attention to what I'm going to tell you today."

You may believe your data or slide deck contains the really good stuff in your presentation. But what exists in those places is the evidence to prove the overall point you're making. When you reveal what you want to share with the audience—and why it's going to make a difference in their lives—that's the reason for your talk. Audience members desperately need to know that, if they're going to sit up, pay attention, and take to heart what you're telling them. The ever-present question, "Why should I care about all of this?" has now been answered in their minds. And it's been decided in your favor.

CLOSE-UP

The Six Rules of Effective Public Speaking

In public speaking, there's a strong relationship between a dynamic performance and success. In fact, the more you can connect with audiences rather than remaining in the comfort zone of your content, the more successful you'll be. Here are my "Six Rules of Effective Public Speaking." They embody the philosophy that *great speaking means great performing!*

Rule #1: Make the Audience the Center of Your Universe

You are not the focus of the event—the audience is. Ultimately, every good speaker cares more about the listeners than himself. This can be a tough prescription to fill if you have speech anxiety, which naturally makes you self-conscious and self-focused. But keeping the audience front and center in your mind actually lifts a huge burden off your shoulders. It prevents you from worrying too much about your performance. The outcome is likely to be much more exciting for listeners. Seeing people enthused by what you are saying is one of the most gratifying experiences that can happen to you as a speaker.

Rule #2: Focus on Relationships

If the audience is the center of your universe, you're already focused on the right task: establishing and maintaining a relationship with them. Your speech›s content can never live on its own—if it could, why would there be a presentation?

Three relationships are going on during a speech: (1) between you and the audience; (2) between you and the content; and (3) between the audience and the content. In the first, you engage listeners and arouse their interest. In the second, you interpret your content for those listeners. And in the third, the audience relates to your content because you've pointed out why it matters to them. Pay attention to all three of these relationships.

Rule #3: Understand Your Purpose

Too many speakers confuse topic and purpose. To the question, "What's your purpose in giving this presentation?" they'll respond with something like: "Well, I'm going to talk about the new software." But that's the *topic*—the information they'll be sharing. It definitely isn't what they want to accomplish (which is this case is probably the steps needed to use the new tool successfully). Audiences have the reasonable hope of being better off for having listened to you. And that's exactly what you must try to make happen. Being clear on your purpose will help you gather exactly the right information (the content) to accomplish it.

Rule #4: Use Your Body

Your body is a powerful communication tool. You're not a brain in a bell jar communicating telepathically! Audiences need you to give *physical expression* to your material. That means understanding how to use body language as a speaker (this topic is covered fully in Chapter 7).

In the meantime, here are three suggestions: 1. Stand rather than sit if you have a choice. Otherwise, you eliminate 50 percent of your physical presence. 2. Come out from behind the lectern, which is a physical obstacle. 3. Make your gestures few in number, saving each one for when you *really* want to emphasize a point.

Rule #5: Become Vocally Expressive

Your voice is the most flexible speaking tool you own aside from the brain itself. The voice is capable of a wide range of coloration and effects. They include astonishment, incredulity, skepticism, joy, disappointment, and a few hundred other emotional and intellectual responses.

To speak without vocal variation or color means using a "mono" or single tone, from which we derive the derogatory word **monotonous**. If you're limited vocally, work with a speech coach. He or she can show you the vocal dynamics that will make you a more exciting speaker.

Rule #6: Boost Your Skills at Q & A

I call Q & A "the forgotten avenue of audience persuasion." Virtually anyone can give a reasonably good presentation if they've practiced enough. But what happens when the questions, challenges, and pushback begin? That's when it becomes obvious to everyone whether the speaker really knows their stuff.

If you can handle this challenging segment of your talk with poise, knowledge, style, and a bit of self-deprecating humor, you'll truly embody leadership presence. Get good at Q & A!

HOW TO TURN YOUR PASSION
INTO A POWERFUL SPEECH

Let's say you're totally committed to your topic and message. And you're equally focused on getting the audience to understand everything in a way that relates to their lives. To accomplish that last task, you face a high hurdle: speaking in a way that not only aids listeners' comprehension, but that conveys emotionally what you're trying to say. If you've ever seen a speaker who is overly emotional, you'll understand how unbridled passion can overwhelm anything else being conveyed. You need to know, in other words, how to *manage* your performance so you can turn your passion into a powerful speech without upsetting the balance between raw emotion and professionalism.

In doing so, you may face another problem, which is common to too many speakers: relying on your content to persuade and motivate people. In other words, leaving your own emotion and commitment off stage.

There's an old Irish proverb that says, "You'll never plow a field by turning it over in your mind." I think of that saying sometimes when the passion involved in a speech seems to live only in the written words, not in the performance. An audience can't see and hear your commitment by osmosis. If you don't *display* how you feel, how are you going to get them to believe as strongly in your viewpoint as you do?

Your speech's words, slides, and displays can only accomplish so much. Yes, data points can convey information efficiently. But all the rest of it—including the immediacy of your message, its benefit for listeners, and the actual meaning of what you're saying—is solidly *your territory* as speaker.

How, then, can you turn your passion into a powerful speech that reaches people emotionally as well as intellectually?

Just Talk to Us ... and Stop Trying to Be Perfect

There's an aspect of public speaking that I urge you to avoid. It's called "perfectionizing." It means what it sounds like: attempting to create a beautifully polished presentation that's perfect in every respect. This is due partly to what I discussed earlier: spending too much time crafting a beautiful literary document prior to your speech. The public speaking realm is more boxing ring than literary salon; your job is not to give a recital, but to step inside the ropes and mix it up.

Trying to write a perfect speech is useless for three reasons:

1. You probably can't do it unless you're a talented speechwriter.
2. You'll get wrapped up in the rhythms of writing, which are different from those of speaking.
3. It will keep your attention on your script rather than on listeners' moment-by-moment response.

Believe me, audiences really don't care about beautiful rhetoric. They do care about speakers who can connect with them and who seem to share their interests and values. Think of why you voted for a political candidate and you'll understand this last part immediately. A solid punch to the gut is more productive than gently stroking someone's sensibilities. When it comes to moving an audience, you need to be as adept on your feet as you are with your pen.

Learn the Actor's Skill of Externalizing What You Feel

Once you commit to speaking with impact rather than oratory, it's time to learn how to get it across the footlights.

My clients often hear me say it's never a question of having passion or even a fierce desire to share your feelings with listeners. It always comes down to *demonstrating who you are in performance*. Audiences aren't mind readers—if you don't show it, they won't know it.

Here's where you must take a page from the actor's art. Actors spend their entire careers learning how to externalize what characters are thinking and feeling. The reason, of course, is so that audiences understand what that character is going through in the context of the drama (or comedy). So, here's a quick-study guide on four ways to externalize what's inside you when you speak so that audiences "get" it:

THE ART OF 'EXTERNALIZING' FOR PUBLIC SPEAKING

1. Turn your energy around: Perfectionizing speakers think in terms of their own performance. But you're not the sun in the public speaking solar system! That's the audience. In effect, they are the center of everything and you are in motion around them—not the opposite. And like the sun, your audience is the source of all your energy. The simple act of turning your energy outward to listeners rather than inward toward yourself will allow you to have more of a relationship with listeners than with your notes or slides.

2. Think in terms of physical expression: Most of us are guilty of Talking Head Syndrome. You know this malady: the speaker stands statue-like behind the lectern, or monument-like at the conference table, though the lips appear to be moving. We experience a static presence going on and on about the content. A vital tool of connection between human beings—the body—is left offstage!

Stiff and lifeless performances like that leave the speaker's engagement invisible. Since audience members don't have a crystal ball, they need you to physically express what you're saying. *Body language makes everything you say stronger.* Its elements—posture, stance, gestures, facial expressions, eye contact, and the voice (which is produced physically)—are there to help you express yourself fully. Effective body language will raise your performance to an entirely new level. Physical expressiveness is one of the keys to being memorable.

3. Mind the pace and shape of your speech: Nothing is worse than an interesting topic diluted through a speech that lacks shape or pacing. Think of a desert: the land stretching away in every direction without anything to break the monotony. That's what a featureless speech looks like to an audience. Memorability in speaking means giving a talk exactly the way you intend it to come across. Your pace must be comfortable for you while allowing listeners to relax and absorb what you say.

   You also need to consider the shape of the talk. Which segments of your speech should have the greatest impact? What are the most dramatic parts? Where should the climax occur—for instance, the part where you state the problem most powerfully, or the moment you reveal the solution? The parts of your speech aren't equal. You should know how to play up the major sections while downplaying the others.

4. Use your performance area: The space in which you stand as a speaker—from convention stage to a few square feet at the end of a conference table—is yours to command. This too is an aspect of speaking memorably. As audiences, we expect you to move—to use the space itself to emphasize things you're saying. Don't prowl or wander; but move with a purpose tied to what you're trying to achieve at each moment. Even a lectern shouldn't stop you from conveying your passion in a powerful way. Stand behind it and refer to your notes when that's necessary. But take opportunities to come out from behind it. You'd be amazed at how doing that makes your speech come to life—for you *and* the audience.

CAN WE HAVE A CONVERSATION?

When you take the steps that I've just outlined, you'll come across as a more confident and memorable speaker. At the same time, there are some more subtle aspects of a winning speaking style you need to be aware of. I'm talking about speaking with simplicity, clarity, and a conversational tone, and being seen as likable.

As a speaker you should always try to speak simply and clearly. One of history's most creative thinkers, Leonardo da Vinci, said, "Simplicity is the ultimate sophistication." The most famous speakers in our language left an historical legacy because plain speaking rings in their phrases. Here are some examples:

- Abraham Lincoln's "government of the people, by the people, for the people."
- Winston Churchill's "never in the field of human conflict was so much owed by so many to so few."
- Martin Luther King, Jr.'s "I have a dream."
- Sojourner Truth's "Ain't I a Woman?"

Great speeches—and remarkable presentations—contain far more 'nickel' than 'dollar' words. Anglo-Saxon's concrete direct quality usually has more impact than Latin's flowery oration. The greatest thoughts are always expressed most simply, because simple language can be understood by everyone.

Consider this excerpt that shows the power of simple language. Corporate speechwriter Richard Dowis wrote it:

Short words can make us feel good. They can run and jump and dance and soar high in the clouds. They can kill the chill of a cold night and help us keep our cool on a hot day. They fill our hearts with joy, but they can bring tears to our eyes as well. A short word can be soft or strong. It can sting like a bee or sing like a lark. Small words of love can move us, charm us, lull us to sleep. Short words give us light and hope and peace and love and health—and a lot more good things. A small word can be as sweet as the taste of a ripe pear, or tart like plum jam. Small words make us think. In fact, they are the heart and soul of clear thought.[4]

Did you notice that this 141-word passage consists of only one-syllable words?

When you make your words simple and clear, you have a *conversation* with your audience. That's a key to successful public speaking. Why? Because both you and your listeners are at your best when you are conversing with each other. That's when you are most natural and least self-conscious. Isn't the thought of having a conversation with someone less intimidating than an upcoming speech?

Because you're at ease in a conversation, you look and sound more like yourself. Almost certainly, you gesture and color your voice in a way that's much closer to the real you than during "public speaking." You're relaxed, and it shows—so you're much better at expressing genuine passion and empathy. Any audience hearing you in that vein will relax into the conversation, becoming more open and receptive. Why wouldn't they? If you're genuine and enthused about your topic you'll be more enjoyable to listen to than if you're trying to be a good speaker.

Can You 'Chat' About Important Things?

There's another reason being conversational is vital to speaking today. Television—and now online video meetings—have changed the game. TV started it all by bringing people into everyone's living room. Suddenly, performers weren't speaking from public stages with us in the audience. From news anchors to game show hosts, they were in our homes. And they became very good at being conversational—at just *chatting* with us—because their professions demanded it. Mass communication became closer and warmer and more casual than it had ever been before.

These days experts and everyday people alike chat with us via Zoom meetings, webinars, podcasts, and FaceTime. We even see them fumbling to press the right button to get things started... why, they're just like us!

The result is that more than ever we expect speakers to be conversational, even about important issues. Watch a video of John F. Kennedy's inaugural speech from 1961 and compare it with a speech on the same occasion by any of our recent presidents. You may be struck by how far we've come toward conversational public speaking, even in highly formal settings. All of this means that to connect with listeners—no matter how vital your topic or high-profile your appearance—you must strike a balance between professionalism and having a conversation with those on the other end.

And it's important to be likable too. The speech coach to President Ronald Reagan (who possessed some charm as a speaker) called likability a "magic bullet," and considered it a critical factor in speaking success. "If your audience likes you," he said, "they'll forgive just about everything else you do wrong. If they don't like you, you can hit every rule right on target and it doesn't matter."[5]

Get an audience to like you, and they will more likely enjoy being in your company. They will want you to succeed. Many business presenters keep their distance from the audience because they're more attuned to their content than to listeners. You need to go in exactly the opposite direction. If it's clear to people that you care deeply whether they understand—and if you're working at establishing a relationship with them—they'll sense something happening in the room. It will seem to them like a shared experience. And indeed, it will be. They'll think of this speech as something memorable. If that happens, it's guaranteed that they will think the same of you.

HOW TO MAKE YOUR SPEECHES EXCITING

Now let's go one step further—by making your speeches exciting.

First, let's discuss an essential component of the learning experience for anyone listening to a speech. It's really an amplifier in terms of how your speech is received (and how you are perceived). It's *dopamine.*

Dopamine is a neurotransmitter released in the brain when you experience a reward of some kind. If you discover something new and interesting, dopamine is released. Similarly, if you're setting out on an adventure (as an exceptional speaker will get audience members to feel), again, dopamine is present. Thrill-seekers, gamblers, and those addicted to chemical substances crave this strong stimulus-and-reward response.

So do *learners*—provided that they perceive what they're being taught as new and exciting. Those experiences then become "sticky" and therefore memorable. And conversely, where dopamine levels remain low, the experience is eminently forgettable. As neuroscientist Martha

Burns tells us, "the more motivated and interested we are in an activity the more dopamine is released and the better we remember it." She recommends the acronym NEAR to understand this response: New, Exciting, and Rewarding.[6]

Now think about this in terms of public speaking. A major reason most presentations are forgettable is because the speaker plays it safe. He or she may think, "Presentations are *always* done this way in this industry, and so I'm going to go along." Basically, these speakers are hoping to get through their talk with their skin intact. Doesn't sound like a new, exciting *or* rewarding approach, does it?

Of course, just as with financial investments, your tolerance for risk plays a part in terms of how far you as speaker are willing to go in terms of newness and creating excitement. But at least think about how you might do things differently!

If a slide deck is used in every presentation in your department, what would happen if you didn't use one in yours? Or vice versa. Other questions to ask yourself: "What would my talk be like if it were shorter than the norm, or conversely, more comprehensive?" "Would some discussion between me and the audience be productive?" "What might happen if this became a team presentation rather than just me speaking?" "What if I invited an audience member on stage for a demonstration?"

Any of these approaches—or others you might come up with on your own—may seem like a new path forward to an audience. To make a presentation more exciting and rewarding, base your approach as closely as possible on the needs of the group. Remember, your goal is always to help listeners be better off for having listened to you. The best way to be memorable isn't to be considered a smooth talker. It is to improve your listeners' lives in some small or big way.

And have fun! To see how being excited yourself can help make you compelling to watch, catch Hans Rosling or Benjamin Zander in their passionate TED talks.

HOW TO PREPARE AND PRACTICE

What about the key area of preparation and practice for more memorable speaking? Here two factors are of particular importance: (1) having a positive mindset and (2) preparing the right way just before you go on.

British theatrical voice coach Cicely Berry quotes a line from T.S. Eliot's poem "Ash Wednesday" in this regard: 'Teach us to care and not to care.' "The 'caring' is the work done to prepare," she says, "and the 'not caring' is letting it go."[7]

In other words: do all the work necessary to understand your listeners and what you want to accomplish. Then let it go, trusting in the moment of performance to make it happen. Too many presenters never 'let go.' Instead, they continue to focus only on their content, often fretting about getting all their material in during the time allowed. The result is that they're not thinking about the audience and what they need to do to get through to them!

The Power of the Words You Choose

If you want to become a more memorable speaker, don't remain chained to the same old topics you always talk about in your practice sessions. Trying practicing with "heightened" material such as poetry, Shakespeare, or great historical speeches. You'll gain an appreciation for the meaning and power of words, along with the rhythms of rich and evocative language.

For one thing, you'll discover that part of the power of language is in the sounds of the words themselves. (Working with anything from Shakespeare will really make you aware of this effect.) Just as music reaches us in ways that are deeper than our conscious thoughts, so does effective language. Consider how interesting it might be for an audience if you ditched clichéd business phrases ("bottom line," "buckets," and "leaving money on the table" come effortlessly to mind). What if you used descriptive words that are more successful at conveying the *exact* meaning of your thoughts?

For instance, let's take those three phrases I used above as examples. "The bottom line is…" can become a rhetorical question (a great device for breaking up a one-way talk and refreshing listeners' interest): "So where does that leave us in terms of our choices at this point?" "Buckets" can easily become groups (or groupings) or "actions based on priority." And if you've left money on the table, then you've obviously failed to follow-up, close, take advantage of an opening, act decisively, seize the moment, etc.

Vocal aspects, i.e., how you deliver the phrases, also has a part to play in memorable performances. If you sense in your practice sessions, for instance, that it's all becoming stale and won't work in front of an audience, remember this (also from Berry): Your voice will never be as good in practice as when you've completed and forgotten the exercises. Instead, at the moment of performance, you will use your voice with imagination.[8] You will, that is, if you're in the moment and intent on getting through to people rather than delivering information!

For instance, it's not unusual for one of my clients to say in a training session: "If I'm struggling like this now, how am I going to do well in front of an audience?" I usually reply: "Oh, you're going to be much better in performance! It will be the real situation, in front of the actual audience. You'll bring your best game. What we're doing here is just a poor simulation."

A Word About What to Do Just Before You Go On: This is an important moment that many speakers make more difficult for themselves. That's because they get into the wrong mindset. How about you? Do you spend valuable about-to-go-on time concerning yourself with getting the information across *just so*?

It is much more productive to use this time to get centered, and to remind yourself of who you are about to speak to and what you want to achieve with them. To explain further, I'll use a theatrical metaphor.

Imagine it's opening night of a play and you're standing in the wings listening for the cue to make your entrance. Are you rehearsing your lines one last time? You'd better not be!

Do that and you just might freeze in front of hundreds of people, allowing the result you were trying to prevent to occur. As every actor understands, if you don't know your lines by now, you won't help yourself by frantically trying to recall them just before the curtain goes up. What you should be thinking about is what your character was doing a moment ago and where he or she is coming from, so you're a real person walking onto the set, with a whole life behind the lines you're about to say.

The public speaking situation is no different, because you either know your content by now or you don't. You should be asking yourself questions about the audience. Who are they, what are their needs concerning this presentation, and most important, how will you connect with them?

You won't lose one bit of the material at your command. Equally important, you'll be someone who is present for the audience. Isn't that more memorable than a speaker who appears to be anxious about delivering the content perfectly?

CLOSE-UP

The 7 Key Components of Effective Presentations

Great speaking isn't only about performance, of course. If you want your message to resonate and to persuade audiences, you need to understand what goes into a successful talk. That means a strategy for moving people combined with a strong structure of the speech itself. You can then combine those two elements with successful execution.

Below are my *7 Key Components of Effective Presentations*. Learn them and you'll be well on your way to transforming data delivery into the gold standard of a memorable talk.

1. **The Greeting.** Speakers often neglect an appropriate audience greeting—in other words, rushing right into the content. Greeting your listeners is essential for five reasons: (1) It's your first and best opportunity to establish rapport; (2) Your audience is paying maximum attention at this point; (3) Your credibility and the audience's trust in you start here; (4) It establishes your tone and "flavor" as a speaker; and (5) You demonstrate you're going to be interesting…or not.

   To make this speech moment work, make sure you establish solid eye contact. (Stop looking down at those notes!) And know exactly what you're going to say. Never wing it.

2. **The Grabber.** You need to *compel* your audience's attention at the start. Avoid the boring "Today I'm going to talk about" opening. Instead, cast off with something that hooks listeners. It's not hard—speakers have been doing it for thousands of years. A question, story, statistic, startling statement, visual image, or other grabber you may come up with will work. This moment of your speech—right after your greeting—is like a rocket launch:

either it gets your presentation off the ground successfully or it doesn't.

3. **A Preview of Your Speech.** Once you've grabbed your audience's attention, let them in on what specific aspects of the topic you're going to address. Have you ever heard someone speak so that five minutes into the talk you say to yourself, "What's this about?" People will be much more comfortable if they know where you and they are headed together. Follow the great self-help guru Dale Carnegie's advice: Tell the audience what you're going to say, say it; then tell them what you've said. Here's an acronym that might help: B-L-U-F, or Bottom Line Up Front. Let the audience know the point you're here to make, then show them the reasons why this is so.

4. **Your Main Points, with Evidence.** Develop your points logically backing up each one with *evidence*. Otherwise, it's all just your opinion. Why should listeners believe you more than the next person? They will once you give them compelling evidence! It can take many forms: expert opinion, personal anecdote, statistic, client testimonial, case study—the list is as long as whatever supports your argument. And don't forget transitions. *You* know how your main points fit together, but your audience doesn't. Make sure they understand how the segment you were just talking about is related to the one you're about to begin discussing. (You'll find more on transitions on page 58.)

5. **Vivid and Visual Language.** If there's an orphan in the public speaking family, it's the science of linguistics, or using words effectively. A word can either denote (refer to explicitly) or connote (suggest an association). Of the two, connotations are much more evocative because they can be emotionally powerful. For instance, my New World Dictionary tells me that "female parent" is explicit and serviceable enough; but "mother" connotes love, caring, tenderness, and a world of positive associations. *Use language that awakens emotional connotations.* Metaphors, similes, and comparisons are great for this. Think of Churchill's "iron curtain." When you look at great speakers, you'll see how many of them are good at speaking metaphorically.

6. **Transitions.** It's surprising how many speakers ignore transitions. But audiences need them to connect the different segments of a speech. Logical and easy-to-follow presentations have clear transitions! One solution is to use an *internal summary* (summing up what you were just talking about) followed by an *internal preview* (revealing what's coming next). For example, "Now that we've seen _____, let's look at how that translates into improved efficiency concerning _____." Make it easy for listeners to follow your thinking!

7. **The Clincher.** Just as your opening needs a *grabber*, you can seal the deal with a powerful *clincher*. Your closing is a priceless opportunity to be memorable, so don't neglect it. Don't just recap your main points, though—give listeners something new and interesting so your ending becomes "sticky." What you say here should help your speech resonate with listeners long after you've finished speaking. To create a good clincher, ask yourself: "What can I say to finish that will keep my message in everyone's mind?" Here's an important hint: the same rhetorical devices that work as grabbers (e.g., question, story, statistic) can be effective as clinchers. Just try not to use the same approach in both your opening and closing.

CHAPTER 4

Overcoming Nerves and Speaking with Confidence

> There's an old story about an actor testifying in court.
> The prosecutor says to the actor on the stand:
> "Sir, who is the greatest actor of all time?"
> The actor says, "Me."
> The attorney says, "Isn't that a bit egotistical?"
> The actor replies, "Perhaps. But I'm under oath."
>
> —*As reported by Roger Ailes*

Can you develop that actor's level of confidence when you speak in public? Maybe not—but then, you don't need to. Your task isn't to be the world's best. It is to sincerely and honestly share a topic that you know something about with us. In fact, sincerity is one of the most important elements in a speech. If you are truly concerned with helping us to understand—much more than caring about your own success—it will be easier for you to reach and genuinely connect with us, no matter how large an audience we make up. You'll be more relaxed, less self-conscious, and not so anxious to please. You will both feel and display more confidence.[1]

Unfortunately, too many people are focused on avoiding failure. The numbers regarding public speaking stage fright, in fact, are staggering. It's been said that between 70 and 75 percent of Americans report fear of public speaking.[2] The current population of the U.S. is 328 million. If one out of every ten people with speech phobia suffers truly serious anxiety that adds up to nearly 23,000,000 Americans with this problem. That's twenty-three *million*.

And then there's the rest of the world.[3]

Yet, not only is there hope for you if you suffer from stage fright—but you have all the resources within you to become a more comfortable and confident speaker. Let me share several extraordinary examples of people I've coached who overcame staggering anxiety to speak with great success.

Peter Dhu is a gentleman from Perth, Australia who suffered from a truly debilitating stutter. Peter's stutter was so bad that he was called "Dumb Peter" in school. And when he graduated college and became a medical researcher, his boss took him aside one day and said, "Peter, I don't know if there's a future in this profession for you, because you don't speak." But Peter not only learned to speak in spite of his stutter—today he's a motivational speaker on leadership! He gives keynotes around the world, sharing his experience with other motivational speakers about how to grow their businesses.

As part of his talk, Peter shows an amazing video of him in his medical researcher days, when he's asked by someone off-camera to state his name and address. For a full minute (a very long reign of silence in a video), Peter struggles just to give the name of his street, and isn't able to do it. Comparing Peter today—a poised and confident motivational speaker—with the struggling young man in the video is compelling proof that anyone can learn to speak more confidently.

A speaker who had an entirely different problem is a client I'll call Mary. Mary came to me for coaching for a mother-of-the-groom toast she would be giving at her son's wedding reception. She told me before we started working together—and I had already noticed—that she had a neurological condition resulting in a pronounced head tremor. At our training facility in Boston, Mary practiced her toast, and I videotaped it.

When we watched the video together a few minutes later, Mary was aghast. She couldn't believe how noticeable her uncontrollable head movement was. I tried to reassure her—telling her it didn't really matter, and reminding her that most of the people at the reception would know about it. I also tried to convince her that what the guests would be interested in would be her sentiments about her son and his new bride, not her physical demeanor. But she wasn't having any of it. She declared: "No. I'm going to give this speech without my tremor."

I thought this was clearly impossible, though I didn't say that. And anyway, she wasn't going to be denied. So, we did it again.—And for the full five minutes of her toast, Mary's head was steady as a rock. I was flabbergasted. And I thought to myself: "If this isn't evidence of how a person's determination to overcome a poor speaking performance can make a difference, I don't know what is."

Are You Facing a 'Mountain of Anxiety'? Some of us don't experience speaking anxiety. When we do, however, we tend to see eventual success in overcoming this problem as a mountain that's too high to climb. There's a reason speech anxiety or *glossophobia* is the most prevalent form of social anxiety. It puts you front-and-center in a harsh spotlight where literally everyone is staring at you. You have to do or say something—and you have to do it *now*. There aren't too many life situations when the pressure to deliver meets our self-perceived inadequacies in such a succeed-or-die moment.

At least, that's the way our mind works if we suffer from speech fear. But it really isn't that desperate or hopeless a situation—not by a long shot. When clients start our Fearless Speaking coaching program at The Genard Method, I tell them the aim is not only to reduce their fear while improving their skills. It's also to allow them to *enjoy* public speaking and to look for opportunities to do it more. That's usually when they laugh or roll their eyes. Yet Peter and Mary, described above, are living proof that this kind of transformation happens every day—even in serious cases like theirs. In fact, it's not unusual for a client to contact me months or even years after completing the program to tell me how much they now enjoy speaking in public!

CLOSE-UP

4 Dangerous Public Speaking Myths

Do you know the saying, "We're our own worst enemy"? It certainly is true when it comes to being nervous and overly self-conscious on stage. Even worse is when we buy into some of the myths that have cropped up about public speaking. And what a shame! These fantasies can keep us from seeking out opportunities to speak in public and get our voices heard. Here are four of the worst statements you should never believe.

Myth #1: Public speaking is dangerous. This is a particularly damaging myth. Not only are audience members never your enemy. But even a failed presentation will rarely result in your being fired, demoted, or even seriously compromised in your job. Public speaking just isn't as perilous as any of the things that really should scare us, no matter how hard we might try to make it so. Remember: a diamond is formed by pressure. Only afterwards does it get polished and become brilliant. If you find that speaking in public is challenging, it's also a golden opportunity for you to grow.

Myth #2: Nervousness will make you perform poorly. Where's the link between feeling jitters and demonstrating that you don't know what you're talking about? There isn't one…unless, of course, you really *don't* know your stuff! And if that's the case, it's not an issue of speaking fear at all. Although nervousness can make you feel ill at ease it's such an internal state that it doesn't easily transfer to your skill set. Stories are common from both business and theater where someone will come offstage and say to a colleague, "Oh, I was horrible. I was so *nervous!*" Most of the time the other person will respond, "Really? I didn't see anything. I thought you were really good."

Myth #3: Everyone will see how nervous you are. And once the audience sees that, they will realize that YOU CAN'T DO YOUR JOB! This is nonsense. Most nervousness isn't visible because, as I mentioned above, it's an internal state. And if the audience does see that you're nervous, they're likely to sympathize because they know that public speaking can be nerve-racking. Audiences feel good when you succeed and embarrassed when you fail. They actually want you to do well, because no one wants to be embarrassed! And anyway, they really are paying attention to what you're saying (rather than you) if they think your message is worthwhile.

Myth #4: You have to be an excellent speaker. Says who? If you make your living as a motivational speaker, your performance should be exceptional. But for everyone else, it doesn't need to. Your job is to be a good manager, salesperson, Chief Medical Officer, etc., and you need to be a good communicator as part of your job. And that's enough. Trying to be "excellent" hinders your ability to be effective because it confuses polish with virtue. Your task is to connect with listeners and deliver value—not to be slick, charismatic, or a stand-up comic. Instead of trying to occupy the top public speaking tier, concern yourself with being honest and trustworthy. If you know your stuff, you will give your audience something valuable. That's what constitutes true excellence.

DO YOU HAVE STAGE FRIGHT?

So, how about you personally—what's your level of stage fright? Everyday nervousness and butterflies in the stomach are perfectly normal responses to an upcoming speech. In fact, they are beneficial, since they get you ready for the big game (and also make you more likely to do your homework)!

But when your level of concern and self-consciousness veers from jitters to anxiety, it's time to take some action. That can include a wide range of interventions. As a start, remember that your response may be different from someone else's, so you need your own plan of action.

For instance, a high level of anxiety days or weeks ahead of time is different from a panic attack that hits the moment you see the audience. And that feeling isn't the same as someone who doesn't worry beforehand and doesn't get panicked, but has an unpleasant physical reaction to the speaking situation. Determining where you fall on the "speech anxiety meter" is vital.

Below is an instrument that can help you gain some perspective. It's the "Stage Fright Quiz" from my book *Fearless Speaking: Beat Your Anxiety, Build Your Confidence, Change Your Life.* The quiz consists of thirty questions about how you react to speaking in public. It includes three types of reactions: (1) learned responses, (2) anticipatory behavior, and (3) anxiety that occurs while you're delivering your speech. Once you've answered the questions, you'll score yourself on a scale that includes four levels of stage fright: low, moderate, significant, and high.

See where you come out on the stage fright scale using this measurement tool. Afterwards, you'll be able to look more closely at your own brand of speaking anxiety, so you can do something about it.

THE STAGE FRIGHT QUIZ

Please circle the appropriate number for each of your responses:

1 = Strongly disagree
2 = Disagree
3 = Neutral
4 = Agree
5 = Strongly agree

Learned Behavior (10 Questions)

I'm comfortable speaking to small groups but uncomfortable in front of large audiences.

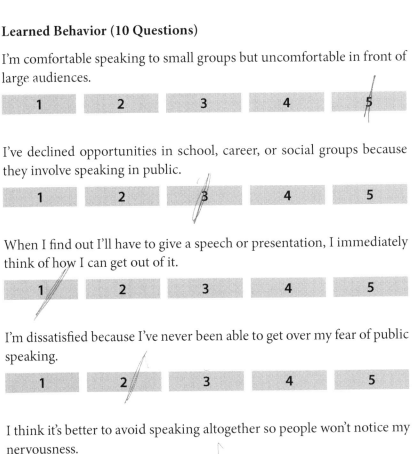

| 1 | 2 | 3 | 4 | 5 |

I've declined opportunities in school, career, or social groups because they involve speaking in public.

| 1 | 2 | 3 | 4 | 5 |

When I find out I'll have to give a speech or presentation, I immediately think of how I can get out of it.

| 1 | 2 | 3 | 4 | 5 |

I'm dissatisfied because I've never been able to get over my fear of public speaking.

| 1 | 2 | 3 | 4 | 5 |

I think it's better to avoid speaking altogether so people won't notice my nervousness.

| 1 | 2 | 3 | 4 | 5 |

A negative experience in the past where I experienced failure while performing has stayed with me.

1	2	3	4	5

I've been unable to fully enjoy an otherwise happy occasion because I had to get up and say something.

1	2	3	4	5

I dread it when everyone around the table or the room has to introduce themselves.

1	2	3	4	5

At times I wanted to contribute to a discussion but didn't because of self-consciousness.

1	2	3	4	5

I think I'll look foolish or that people will lose respect for me if I get up to speak.

1	2	3	4	5

Anticipatory Anxiety (10 Questions)

If I have a speech or presentation coming up, I worry about it for days or weeks.

1	2	3	4	5

My sleeping habits or mood may be affected.

1	2	3	4	5

I sometimes visualize my speech or presentation going poorly prior to the engagement.

| 1 | 2 | 3 | 4 | 5 |

I tend to over-prepare my materials in case I'm caught without anything to say.

| 1 | 2 | 3 | 4 | 5 |

I'm overly concerned with what people will think about my performance.

| 1 | 2 | 3 | 4 | 5 |

I believe that I'll come across as less knowledgeable than I really am.

| 1 | 2 | 3 | 4 | 5 |

I sometimes think I won't be as good as others who'll be speaking.

| 1 | 2 | 3 | 4 | 5 |

I worry that I'll forget what to say or won't have anything interesting to offer.

| 1 | 2 | 3 | 4 | 5 |

I'm convinced that everyone will see how nervous I am.

| 1 | 2 | 3 | 4 | 5 |

There are meetings or situations that I find particularly stressful to speak at.

| 1 | 2 | 3 | 4 | 5 |

Delivering Your Speech (10 Questions)

My heart starts to pound when it's time to deliver my speech or presentation.

1	2	3	4	5

I often wish I were somewhere else instead of giving this talk.

1	2	3	4	5

I experience feelings of self-consciousness or exposure when I speak in public.

1	2	3	4	5

I pay attention to "how I'm doing" during a presentation rather than staying focused.

1	2	3	4	5

While I'm speaking, I think people don't look interested and are judging me negatively.

1	2	3	4	5

I think the audience will sense that I'm not really a leader or competent enough.

1	2	3	4	5

I'm convinced I'm physically awkward and don't use effective body language.

1	2	3	4	5

I suffer from some or all of these physical sensations: Shortness of breath, dry mouth, sweating, pounding heart, nausea, a shaky voice, being "foggy," or feeling hot and flushed.

| 1 | 2 | 3 | 4 | 5 |

If something goes wrong or I'm asked a tough question, I find it hard to recover and get back on track.

| 1 | 2 | 3 | 4 | 5 |

I find myself becoming preoccupied with my physical symptoms while I'm presenting.

| 1 | 2 | 3 | 4 | 5 |

SCORING:

Below 70 **Low level of stage fright.** You don't suffer from speaking anxiety, and you're likely a high achiever. You'd probably like to maximize your success in speeches, lectures, and presentations, however. Any exercises that allow you to focus and grow your awareness of the speaker-audience connection will help you become a more effective communicator.

70–99 **Moderate level of stage fright.** Some aspects of speaking in public may cause you anxiety, while others probably do not. You will benefit by learning how to harness your energy, strengthen your skills in the areas in which you need improvement, and become a more aware speaker who knows how to control a speaking situation.

100–119 **Significant level of stage fright.** Speech anxiety is a significant part of your approach to speaking situations. You may not have made drastic life and career decisions based on your fear. But you still feel limited in your ability to enjoy speaking and to be successful at it. You could use a toolbox of coping mechanisms for greater control and influence when you speak.

120

120–150   **High level of stage fright.** If you're at this level, you've likely been living with an uncomfortable level of performance anxiety for some time. You probably worry about it excessively and wonder where you can find relief. You need a way to manage your speaking fear and "find a way out" so you can become more confident and comfortable speaking in public.

IS IT ALL IN YOUR MIND?

If you're extremely apprehensive about speaking, in addition to the fear itself you may feel confused. You may understand, for instance, that you're an expert in your field, with years of experience and no problems having conversations about it. Therefore, you may wonder why you go through nervousness or dread over public speaking.

But fear isn't a rational process. It doesn't do any good to tell yourself that your response is all in your mind. It's true that there are powerful neurological reactions that are responsible for some of your fear. Yet emotional and social responses; negative self-talk; and physiological reactions all play a role in how speech anxiety manifests itself.

British voice coach Patsy Rodenburg who works with high-profile actors on the English stage, claims that according to a medical study, "An actor going onstage for a press night [when theater critics and the press are invited] undergoes the same tension as a victim in a major car accident."[4]

That certainly indicates major stress. But it also means major excitement. Let's look, first at how your mind helps create the fearful experience of stage fright, and second, how you can harness your response—in the form of mindfulness—to put yourself in a positive and productive state.

THE BRAIN, EMOTIONS, AND PUBLIC SPEAKING
The Prefrontal Cortex and Limbic System

Homo sapiens, means 'wise' or thinking human being. That attribute—so critical to our nature as a dominant species—can get in our way when we speak in public. That's because it can be hard to turn our powerful brains off!

The executive part of our brain, or *prefrontal cortex,* is designed to control thought, reasoning, emotion, and planning. And in the human brain, it's really massive. The prefrontal cortex takes up nearly one-third of the neocortex or outer layer of the brain. In our nearest relatives the chimpanzee, the prefrontal cortex is only 17% of the neocortex. In a dog, it's 13%, and only 4% in a cat.[5]

Given the role of the prefrontal cortex in our thinking, it's easy to consider this region to be the most important part of our brain. But a critical component of the brain, especially in terms of speaking fear, is the *limbic system,* a C-shaped structure deep in the brain, which is that organ's emotional center. While generating emotional responses, the limbic system also communicates with the centers of higher consciousness, and is involved in instinctive behaviors.[6]

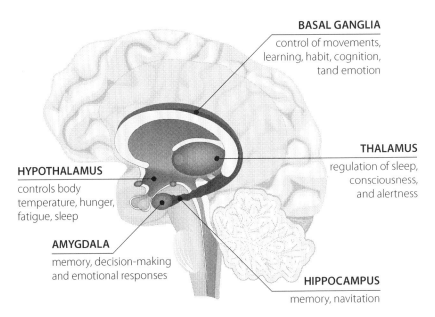

FIGURE 4-1. Limbic system

Limbic 'Memory'

Another function of the limbic system that's important to know for our purposes is its power to embed emotional memories. Pleasant, dangerous, or otherwise significant events in our lives are encoded via the limbic system as encounters we remember—long after the original encoding event. This has particular significance regarding 'learned events' in public speaking. Often, these are negative experiences (frequently but not always occurring when we are young) in which we 'learn' that speaking in public is dangerous, or just something that we don't do well. I call it 'learning to fail.' Significantly, it can undermine our confidence for years after the original event.

One of my clients, for instance, was chosen years ago to deliver a speech to the entire high school in his senior year. He wasn't particularly nervous. But partway through the speech, everything seemed to fall apart and he openly struggled with reaching the end of the talk. He considered the speech a very public failure. From that point on, he was convinced that he wasn't any good at speaking in public.

Another client shared with me her triggering fearful event. When she was a girl, her sister locked her in a closet and left the room for some minutes. It was a terrifying experience because it taught my client how vulnerable she is.

She added hastily after telling me this, "I love my sister dearly, and we're great friends as adults." Yet that event of long ago undermined her confidence in any situation where she feels vulnerable, like getting up in front of others. Notice how in this instance, the initiating event had nothing to do with public speaking. It didn't matter because her limbic brain retained this traumatic emotional memory under a category of 'Situations where I'm vulnerable and should be afraid.'

Let's look more closely at the section of the brain which actually sets off the alarm bells. This is the area that's involved when you suddenly go blank at the opening of a speech, or when you panic and start looking for the exits. It's called the *amygdala*, and it is squarely at the intersection of the public speaking situation and a fearful response to it.

The Amygdala

The amygdala is a small structure in the limbic system whose task is to sort through emotions. (You can see its location in the drawing of the limbic system on the previous page.)

The job of the amygdala is to gather emotional stimuli and determine their significance, including whether a threat is present. It is worth noting, however, that the amygdala's activity doesn't only result in fearful reactions. In its function to get a 'rapid response' going as fast as possible, it doesn't spend time examining the overall situation. It wants to get us to remember our emotional response to interesting phenomena, whether a particular phenomenon is dangerous or merely interesting.

Of course, once we become afraid of something, we are programmed to recall that stimulus in strongly negative terms, and so are from that point on conditioned *toward* that fear.[7] That's what's happening where fear of public speaking is concerned. And it's why we become so agitated in recurring situations that involve speaking to a group.

So even though we've evolved a highly sophisticated thinking and processing brain (the prefrontal cortex), we're still at the mercy of primitive emotions derived from the amygdala any time we sense danger. And we respond quickly and powerfully to what the emotional brain is telling us. Daniel Goleman, the popularizer of emotional intelligence, writes about the direct link between the amygdala and our fear response:

> The amygdala is central to fear. When a rare brain disease destroyed the amygdala (but no other brain structures) in the patient neurologists call "S.M.," fear disappeared from her mental repertoire. She became unable to identify looks of fear on other people's faces, nor to make such an expression herself. As her neurologist put it, "If someone put a gun to S.M.'s head, she would know intellectually to be afraid but she would not feel afraid as you or I would."[8]

Such a powerful stimulus telling us to be afraid can literally be life-saving. However, when it is paired with public speaking, it becomes a problematic response because in those scenarios we're not actually in a life-threatening situation. That makes the amygdala's warning signal an inappropriate reaction, yet one that at the same time can be difficult to overcome. What happens is that you're caught in the dilemma of a brain screaming "Danger!" when the actual speech or presentation isn't a threat to your survival at all.

At any rate, the brain doesn't care. As far as it's concerned, this is the moment to activate your physical mechanism to get you out of danger as fast as possible. And because your survival is at stake (or so your brain perceives), this physiological response takes place at lightning speed.

The amygdala is so good at processing emotional stimuli in fact that it goes into action before you even sense what is happening! The reason is to allow your body to react instantaneously. Once your body has done so, and has completed its kick into high gear, the frontal cortex comes back online. It now begins to process the information received in a more rational process.[9]

"Ah," it concludes, "this isn't really a life-threatening situation at all. It's only public speaking. Okay everybody, stand down."

By this time, however, it's too late to turn off the overwhelming physiological reaction you're going through. You're now smack in the middle of what we know as the "fight or flight response." Stress hormones including epinephrine (adrenalin), cortisol, and norepinephrine have already flooded into your bloodstream. These are powerful chemicals produced by the adrenal gland that prime you for action. Other changes occur. Your pupils dilate; your blood is redistributed to the large muscles you need to fight or flee; and digestion and peristalsis (the forward movement of waste products through the intestines) cease...because you don't have the luxury of dealing with them at the moment.

All of these coordinated responses are wonderfully efficient in terms of getting you to survive rare life-threatening situations. However, if you experience them chronically—through constant speaking fear for instance—they are harmful to the body.

They also make you feel terrible *physically* while you're presenting in front of that audience, while reminding you of how much you hate public speaking. You know the sensations: speeded up and sometimes pounding heart; shallow rapid breathing; dry mouth; shaky voice; light-headedness; even the sensation that the audience is far away—such are the physical reactions that can occur in stage fright. They are, all of them, physiological responses to a dangerous situation when there really isn't one!

Now you're in a truly uncomfortable place. Your prefrontal cortex is trying to rationally sort out what is happening and whether you should be concerned. But the amygdala's alarm has gone off, sending out signals to every major area of the brain. These signals impact the cardiovascular system, muscles, eyes, gut, diaphragm, and lungs: all systems you need to make you alert and physically responsive to the 'threat'. And the entire process—perception of danger, physiological super-activation, and the thinking brain's attempt to figure out what's happening—takes all of about a second.

Negative Cognitive Bias

In addition to your rapid (and powerful) emotional and physical responses, you may also be dealing with some negative cognitive bias. This refers to the tendency to zero in on possibly negative or dangerous outcomes rather than potentially rewarding ones. Our brains focus at the speed of milliseconds—too fast for us even to be conscious that it's happening—on whatever part of the environment seems important to us. If you are cognitively biased toward negative outcomes, that is if you're constantly looking out for them, you'll be getting an inaccurate picture of the world. In effect, you will see things as hazardous, even dangerous, not because they are so, but because you are expecting them to be that way.[10]

As Hamlet said to his friend Horatio, "There is nothing either good or bad, but thinking makes it so."

There's even a way to measure this. A recent experiment found that people with social anxiety pay more attention to negative faces they encounter than positive ones.[11] If this is true, you can imagine how anxious public speakers may be at the mercy of this bias. They may imagine an entire audience of unfriendly people because they're fixated on a few unwelcoming faces!

CLOSE-UP

The Top 10 Causes of Speech Anxiety

Want an attention-grabber the next time you give a talk? Try this: speech anxiety ranks higher than death as the fear people mention most often! How's that for a widespread form of social anxiety?

That finding is from *The Book of Lists*. A recent web post similarly found that public speaking occupies the third spot in most dreaded encounters.[12] So if you fear speaking in public more than (as were also mentioned) riding an escalator or losing all of your social media contacts, you're still not alone.

As the creator of a coaching program for professionals with speaking fear, I'm often asked why otherwise capable people experience it. Why should someone who is highly qualified in his field suffer from nerves, stage fright, imposter syndrome, and even outright panic attacks when presenting? It doesn't seem to make any sense!

Here is my list of the top 10 causes of speech anxiety. I believe this list shows that in spite of any brain-based responses, stage fright clearly isn't just a problem with your thinking processes. In fact, even the most rational mind doesn't stand a chance when it finds itself in the ring with cold stark fear!

1. **Self-Consciousness in Front of Large Groups.** This is the most frequently cited reason for performance anxiety. I often hear, "I'm fine talking to small groups but large audiences make me really anxious." Two strategies will help: (1) Remember that the people in a large audience are the same ones you talk to individually; and (2) Concentrate on just talking to them, or even chatting, rather than "presenting." As a species, we still haven't evolved to speak comfortably in front of the whole tribe. Think of having a conversation and you'll be more likely to come across as your true self.

2. **Fear of Appearing Nervous.** Are you afraid that you'll look fearful? Many speakers are. If that's your starting point, it's easy to think that everyone will conclude that you don't know your topic. But the two responses aren't linked. When you notice that a speaker is nervous, do you immediately judge her competence—or do you sympathize with being nervous in front of an audience? In just the same way, your audiences will extend you sympathy.

3. **Concern About Others' Judgment.** I have mentioned that people probably aren't judging you. One reason—and I realize it's a tough-love message—is that they really don't care about you. They're there to get something out of your lecture or presentation so they know their time has been well spent. Watching a speaker fail is embarrassing for everyone. Believe me, the audience is actually hoping you'll succeed.

4. **Past Failures.** Public speaking anxiety is often learned behavior, as I discussed on pages 70–71 in the section on limbic 'memory.' That is, at some point in the past you failed, and the seed of self-doubt was planted. But if you know your material and are

prepared this time, today—why would things necessarily go south like they did a long time ago? If you're insistent that it will happen again…well, maybe then it will. The lesson is clear: plan to succeed.

5. **Poor or Insufficient Preparation.** If you haven't done your homework—including analyzing the needs of your audience—there's no reason you should succeed. Blame nobody but yourself. Nothing undermines public speaking confidence like being unprepared. But conversely, nothing gives you as much confidence as being ready. So be ready!

6. **Narcissism.** This is the toughest-love message I give to clients who fear public speaking. Indulging in extreme self-consciousness during any activity is narcissistic. When it comes to speaking in front of an audience, how can you influence them if you're totally wrapped up in yourself? You can't. So, turn your full attention and generosity toward your listeners. They matter. You don't.

7. **Dissatisfaction with Your Abilities.** Okay, this is a legitimate concern. But it's also one of the easiest of these top 10 causes of speech anxiety to remedy. You should feel dissatisfied if your speaking skills are below par. But that can be a terrific motivator! Get some speech training. Just knowing you have first-rate skills will give you a truckload of confidence. It will also make you much more eager to speak.

8. **Discomfort with Your Own Body.** Why is it that many of us are physically at ease with family, friends, and team members, but become self-conscious and awkward in front of an audience? If that's you, remember that having a conversation with listeners puts you in a different place from P-R-E-S-E-N-T-I-N-G, when everyone is staring at you and you are super-conscious of the fact. Here's a helpful hint: pay attention to how you hold yourself, move, and gesture when you're surrounded by friends and are at your ease. Then recreate those natural movements (which are you in action) when you're in front of a larger group. Keep in mind: that's exactly the person they came to hear!

9. **Poor Breathing Habits.** Unless you've been trained as an actor or legit singer, you're probably unaware of how to breathe for speech. Public speaking requires more air than passive breathing in order to project the sound over a larger physical area. Also, you need to control your exhalation so you sustain the sound through the end of the idea. And of course, some of those ideas will be complex and take more time (and breath) to express. Even more pertinent to this chapter on overcoming negative thinking and the physical responses to fear: more relaxed breathing helps slow down your galloping heart. Make slower, deeper breathing your new habit.

10. **Comparing Yourself to Others.** Don't do it! As I said earlier in this chapter, your job is never to be an excellent speaker. It is to be interesting when you discuss any topic and good at communicating with people. That's it. The really good news is that nobody in the entire universe can tap into your personal take on the subject as well as you can. Truly, you're the one we came to hear.

BEATING YOUR ANXIETY AND BUILDING CONFIDENCE

So, what can you do if speech anxiety or nervousness are affecting your career or even your quality of life? I will now discuss two of the most powerful ways you can gain the control you need. You'll do so by a) enlisting your brainpower and b) learning how to reach a place of calm serenity. Doing the first involves cognitive restructuring; and the second means practicing controlled and mindful breathing.[13]

CHANGING YOUR NEGATIVE THINKING

One point that's absolutely essential to understanding speaking fear or discomfort is that your performance doesn't change who you are as a person. A poor showing doesn't mean that you suddenly know less about your job or your topic.

It won't, for instance, wipe away your years of dedication as a working professional or amateur enthusiast.

What *is* worth taking to heart is that it's time to change your mind-set when it comes to speaking in public. You need to go from a negative and self-undermining way of looking at speaking, to a more positive and even joyful attitude.

In one sense, you create your own fearful response if you have anxiety over public speaking. That's because there is never as much danger or risk as you think there is. Your anxiety is leading you down a path with no exit. Partly that's because you're substituting your fears for more accurate measurements of your success. Therefore, you create a false reality that's much harsher than the actual speaking situation!

Reorganizing your negative thinking, then, is key to overcoming speech anxiety. This process is called *cognitive restructuring*. That simply means going from a negative mindset to a positive one where public speaking is concerned. Another way to say this is that you'll be changing your role from being your own worst enemy when you speak to becoming your own best friend. Since no one knows more about your negative way of thinking than you do, you can become very good at this process!

Table 4-1 will help you get started. It gives you examples of going from negative self-talk to positive coping statements. It also provides room for you to write in your own personal responses. If you identify with any of the examples given, by all means use them. Or add your own instances of negative self-talk, followed by a corresponding self-validating statement instead. Use the final list to start your own process of positive-based cognitive restructuring.

ADDITIONAL RESOURCE

Do you feel that fear of public speaking is limiting your career? You'll find **my proven 12-day self-guided program for eliminating stage fright** in my book *Fearless Speaking*. You can learn more and download a free chapter here:

https://www.genardmethod.com/help-with
-fear-of-public-speaking-and-stage-fright

Or scan the QR Code.

TABLE 4-1. Developing Positive Coping Statements

Negative Self-Talk	Positive Coping Statement
GO FROM THIS:	*TO THIS:*
I'm just not a good public speaker.	▶ I can learn to speak effectively.
They're going to see I'm nervous.	▶ Most nervousness doesn't show.
I'm going to look like a fool.	▶ I'll focus on my important message.
It's going to be a disaster.	▶ I may very well enjoy this. Let's see!
Lots of things could go wrong.	▶ I can handle the unexpected.
This is a make-or-break situation.	▶ I'm lucky to have been given this spot!
People will judge me.	▶ People are hoping to learn something.
What have I gotten myself into?	▶ What do I have to lose?
Everyone's going to be looking at me!	▶ What an opportunity to reach this audience.
I know I'm going to go blank.	▶ I know my stuff, and I've prepared well.
They'll ask tough questions.	▶ Q & A is another learning opportunity for them.
I have to be perfect.	▶ I'll just have a conversation with my listeners.
_____	▶ _____
_____	▶ _____
_____	▶ _____
_____	▶ _____
_____	▶ _____
_____	▶ _____

BREATHING TO CALM AND RELAX YOURSELF

Now let's go from the cognitive side of dealing with speaking anxiety to the physical dimension. Though each of us can manifest stage fright differently in terms of our thinking, we share the same physiological responses. And over the years, I've found that the best and fastest way to counteract that powerful physical reaction is through breath work. In fact, lack of breath control is one of the earliest and strongest indicators of discomfort with public speaking.

For instance, do you hold your breath when you get up to speak in public? Or if you don't actually hold it, do you breathe more rapidly and shallowly when you're in an anxious situation than you do normally? The answer to the last question is almost certainly 'yes.'

Breathing and Anxiety Reduction

You may have noticed that some speakers gasp for breath at times. That's because nerves can make us so focused on trying to survive a perilous situation that we forget to breathe. This response is probably related to the 'freeze' reaction of our ancestors. When these people spotted, say, a saber-toothed tiger turning in their direction, they probably halted *any* movement, including breathing. Like them (remember, we probably haven't evolved out of thcse behaviors), when faced with the 'danger' of having to keep a group of strangers under our control, we may just stop breathing. The gasping reaction that soon occurs is our body sending our brain an urgent message: "We need some oxygen down here!"

This scenario can be turned on its head, however, because your breath is also a potent weapon for reducing your speaking fear. It's all a question of gaining control of the breathing mechanism while activating the calming components of your nervous system.

Activating the Vagus Nerve

As I explained above, your physiological response to what appears to be a dangerous situation is instantaneous and overwhelming. When your survival is at stake, your brain is willing to wait a while to reach full comprehension until your body gets you out of the hazardous situation.

In reality, it takes all of a second or so for your mind to come back online. But that's long enough for your physical response to have cascaded quickly into hyper mode: the pounding heart, rapid breathing, sweating, and the other symptoms I noted above. By the time this occurs, it's too late to do anything about it. The stress hormones are in the bloodstream and it will take some time for them to be absorbed by the body. Concerning the hormone cortisol in particular, this process can take several hours.[14]

The way to counteract this extreme physiological response is to get your body in the right mode *before* the anxiety-provoking situation shows up. That means using the breath to turn on the part of your nervous system that exists to calm you rather than excite you.

That's the *parasympathetic nervous system* or PNS. The opposite mode—the one that's involved in the "fight-or-flight" or activating mechanism—is the *sympathetic nervous system* (SNS). When you're experiencing speaking fear—or a fearful response of any kind—it's the sympathetic nervous system that's in operation. In fact, in such a situation it is working overtime, which is where the fight-or-flight designation comes in. And it lives up to its name during fear of speaking! Your parasympathetic nervous system, on the other hand, is often called the "rest-and-digest" system. If you can learn how to turn it on *before you're in the stress-provoking speaking situation*, it will be much easier for you to call upon it at the moment when you need it most.

What you're actually doing when you turn on the calming mode is activating the **vagus nerve**. This is the longest cranial nerve in the body that runs all the way from the head to the abdominal region. One of its relevant functions (vital for our purposes) is that it helps regulate the heart rate, speeding up the heart slightly each time you inhale, and slowing it down slightly each time you exhale. Equally important, the vagus nerve is also responsible for switching on the parasympathetic "calming" nervous system. And again, it's the act of exhalation that makes this happen. So, the answer to reining in your galloping heart is really a simple one: make your exhalation longer than your inhalation.

The 4-4-6-2 Pattern. You can breathe in a 4-4-6-2 pattern, for instance. This means inhaling for a silent count of four; pausing for the same amount of time; exhaling for a silent count of six; then stopping the process for a count of two. Then begin it all over again, continuing the process for a few minutes.

You may find this breathing pattern *very* relaxing, since it's bringing the parasympathetic system online. And its job as we've seen is to S-L-O-W T-H-I-N-G-S D-O-W-N. Don't do it when you need to be fully alert or operating machinery, of course. And feel free to adjust the duration of any of the numbers if you feel oxygen starved. But if you can learn to use mindful breathing in this simple way, you'll give yourself a powerful tool when anxiety is pressuring you to lose control.

In the next chapter I'll discuss in more detail the process of breathing more productively, especially for better public speaking. In it, you'll learn how to use breath control not only to calm your nerves, but for more focused and powerful performances.

CLOSE-UP

A 5-Minute Technique to Calm Your Fear of Public Speaking

Here's an easy and practical exercise for more aware breathing. It's a way to achieve sufficient relaxation and calmness that takes just five minutes. Yes, you can actually learn to relax in that amount of time! Once you master the technique, you can do it easily, even at a moment's notice, which is actually when you may need it most.

1. **Find a quiet place.** Your office, hotel room at a conference, even your car parked at the speaking venue will do. If all else fails, a bathroom stall can work. All you need is someplace where you can sit in a relaxed position with your feet flat on the floor.

2. **Close your eyes to block out distractions.**

3. **Listen to your breathing for a full minute.** Feel the way breathing nourishes and sustains you. Experience the breath flowing down your throat and filling your lungs as it brings oxygen to every cell in your body.

4. **Now, with your eyes closed focus on a visual image in your mind.** The image should be a simple colored shape—a green circle, yellow square, blue triangle, etc. Choose an object that doesn't have emotional overtones for you, and avoid red as a color.

5. **See that object (shape AND color) with as much clarity as you can.** This will take real sustained concentration. In fact, you may have to do the exercise a few times before you see anything. As you're imagining your object, thoughts, images, or feelings may arise in your mind. Notice them but let them go gently on their way. Keep a calm persistent focus on your image.

Your breathing will become slower and deeper. This is what you're aiming for: you're now in more of a state of mindfulness. When you're ready, open your eyes and slowly stand. Try to maintain this level of calmness and relaxed breathing.

CHAPTER 5

Breathing for Focus and Power

If you have ever had singing lessons, you have heard your teacher say: "You must learn to breathe from here," as she pointed toward your abdominal region. No one argues with a singing teacher.

—*Ken Crannell*

Words are rooted with the breath.

—*Cicely Berry*

in·spi·ra·tion **1.** a breathing in, as of air into the lungs; inhaling. **2.** an inspiring or being inspired mentally or emotionally. **3.** an inspiring influence; any stimulus to creative thought or action (*Webster's New World Dictionary, Second College Edition*).

Are you surprised to hear that the first dictionary definition of "inspiration" has to do with *breathing*? Yet how appropriate. Inspired thinking—and as we'll see, a strong voice to deliver that thinking to listeners—begins with proper breathing!

Of course, life itself also depends on breathing. But clear differences exist between "vegetative breathing" or breathing for life, and breathing for speech. And speaking with leadership presence requires yet another level of joining breath and performance. Excelling at this level involves (1) creating the actual sound of leadership through a well-supported voice, and (2) using the breath for peak performance.

Stage actors, whose breathing techniques are critical to their performances, put it this way: If you're in control of your breathing, you'll likely give a strong performance. And if you're not, you won't. That's a dramatic way of saying that breathing helps determine everything that's going on with you physically and mentally when you're in front of an audience.

Just how important is breathing to being fully present for listeners? It's not a stretch to go beyond a speech or presentation, and associate breath with spirituality and the energy of the universe—all the great yogic and spiritual traditions do so. These traditions view the energy that's linked to breath "not only as the foundation of our existence on this earth but also as the vital unifying link between body, mind, and spirit."[1]

But you don't need to accept the spiritual aspect of breathing to realize that the breath's essence is a vital part of your life at this moment. And also, as you'll see in this chapter, an essential link between speaking, presence, and power.

How You Experience the World

In practical terms, your manner of breathing is linked to the way you experience the world and respond to it. For instance, breathing that is inhibited or constricted leads to constriction in your responses and to disharmony. An everyday example you can easily relate to (and perhaps notice in yourself) is shallow, upper-chest breathing, so common in our stress-filled society. Whether such breathing is due to unconscious bad habits, or not wanting to reveal that you have a tummy (!), the act of limiting the respiration process like this is harmful both physically and spiritually. Breathing in that way is like wearing tightly fitting armor that can stifle your emotional responses, affect how you relate to others, and even block you from growing and evolving.[2] This practice of shallow upper-chest breathing is also harmful to the production of a strong and resonant voice, which I discuss in the next chapter on vocal dynamics.

BREATHING NATURALLY

To understand and use breathing for greater public speaking presence, we have to start with the production of the breath. In other words, as a speaker you have to know how to breathe naturally.

Does that sound strange? The truth is we all breathe naturally when we are babies and toddlers, and probably through childhood. But many of us develop bad habits after those early years. We start breathing in ways that actually work against us when it comes to having a strong stage presence for public speaking.

To breathe properly and productively for the speaking stage, you must practice *diaphragmatic breathing*. This simply means breathing with the help of your diaphragm: the dome-shaped muscle located below your lungs and above your abdomen. The body's natural breathing sequence depends upon the diaphragm. Here's how it works:

When you inhale, your diaphragm moves downward and flattens somewhat, creating room above it for the expanding lungs. As the diaphragm flattens, it descends toward the abdominal area below it. Since the interior of the body has no spare real estate, your abdomen or "belly" has to go somewhere as the diaphragm pushes it out of the way. Since your ribs on each side and spine in the back inhibit any movement in those directions, your belly moves forward. All of this explains why your abdominal wall bulges *outward* slightly when you inhale.

When you exhale, your lungs naturally grow smaller. Now your diaphragm—no longer having to remain flat and out of the way—can rise and return to its relaxed dome shape. Since your belly (i.e., your abdominal area) is no longer being pushed out of the way from above, it too returns to its former position, moving inward. Therefore, each time you *exhale*, your belly goes back in. Figure 5-1 shows the process in action, with arrows representing the direction of movement of air and the diaphragm.

To summarize: your belly moves outward when you inhale, and inward when you exhale. Think of a balloon inflating and deflating and you'll get the picture. The classic example of this diaphragmatic action is a baby lying on its back in a crib: the baby's belly rises and falls noticeably with each inhalation-exhalation cycle.

Practicing Diaphragmatic Breathing

Try it for yourself right now. Stand up or lie down—it doesn't matter which. Breathe slowly and deeply as you notice the movement in your abdominal area.

Does your belly move out (if you're standing) or up (if you're lying down)? If not—if your belly moves *inward* when you inhale—you're

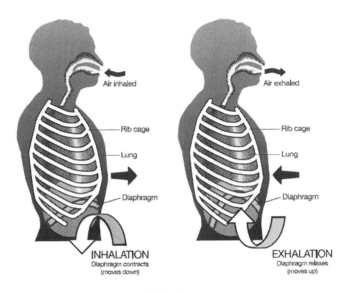

FIGURE 5-1

breathing "backwards." This reverse breathing action isn't harming you in any way, and it isn't all that rare. But it inhibits your diaphragmatic breathing, since it doesn't allow room for your lungs to expand fully once the diaphragm gets out of the way. The diaphragm is actually moving *upward*, which prevents full expansion of the lungs. Therefore, it can leave you less than fully oxygenated when you're speaking.

In other words, breathing in the wrong direction, along with breathing shallowly, keeps your body from gaining a free and effortless reservoir of air! And that is exactly what you need when you're giving a presentation and require a voice that's well supported and projected by breath. If you're in the grip of speech nerves, this whole situation is worsened because you're probably breathing too shallowly to begin with.

It's a simple fact of your anatomy: diaphragmatic breathing provides you with the oxygen you need because your lungs are able to expand fully. That oxygen travels from your lungs into your bloodstream nourishing every cell in your body. It is also the ideal breathing pattern for a well-oxygenated brain while speaking!

In summary, here are the benefits of good diaphragmatic breathing:

The 6 Benefits of Diaphragmatic Breathing

1. Slows your heart rate and centers you psychologically.

2. Provides oxygen to your brain.

3. Aids your stance and appearance.

4. Facilitates good vocal production and "the sound of authority."

5. Supports sound to the *end* of the idea expressed, where the important words come.

6. You appear confident and in control (not gasping or running out of breath).

In the following exercise, you'll practice releasing muscular tension so you can experience effortless diaphragmatic breathing. I suggest lying on a yoga mat or carpet while you do this exercise. The first time you practice the sequence it may take up to 20 minutes to reach the state of calmness described. With more practice, it might take you only 10 minutes to achieve the same level of mental and physical relaxation.

THE PROGRESSIVE RELAXATION EXERCISE

- Lie on your back with eyes closed and arms and feet uncrossed at your sides.

- *Follow your breath:* Be aware of breathing in and out easily. Visualize your breath entering your nose and going down your throat. Stay with the nourishing breath as it passes into your lungs and then throughout your body. Feel how the oxygen nourishes every cell in your body. Become conscious of how refreshing and life affirming each miraculous breath is.

- As you continue to breathe easily, direct your awareness to the top of your head. Be aware of a sense of complete relaxation. As you focus on that area, your scalp and the individual hairs on your head suddenly *release* all tension held within them. You feel a pleasantly heavy sensation like warm lava. Let it move *very* slowly down your head and scalp, gently melting away all tension wherever it reaches.

- Allow that warm, heavy feeling to spread from your scalp to your forehead. Feel the same release of tension, the melting-away, the sensation of smoothness and warmth and relaxation. Continue to experience that sensation in the areas you focused on first.

- Keeping the level of relaxation that you've achieved in your scalp and forehead, let the lava flow down to your eyes. You may hold considerable tension behind your eyes—many people do. Let it melt away.

- Allow the warm melting-lava feeling to slowly proceed down your body. Each part of your body that it reaches immediately relaxes as the tension melts away. When you get to your fingers, allow any remaining tension to flow out of the fingertips. And when you get to your feet, let the same thing happen through your toes. Don't DO anything; just let it happen.

- Once your body is completely relaxed, do a mental scan to locate any remaining pockets of tension. Then let the tightness in those places melt away until you're completely and utterly relaxed. Now, allow your muscles to "remember" what this feels like, i.e., register it in your muscle memory.

- Now that you're totally without tension, place the palm of your dominant hand on your abdomen where it rises and falls with each breath. Breathe gently and deeply. As you do so, feel your hand moving up and down with the "bellows" action of free diaphragmatic breathing. ***This is what natural breathing in a relaxed state feels like.***

BREATHING AND PEAK PERFORMANCE

Why is optimal breathing like this important in improving your stage presence? Practitioners of breathing for yoga, meditation, and mindfulness speak in terms of the overall physical, mental, and spiritual benefits of "breath work." And, they are absolutely right. For our purposes, we need to understand the dramatic ways that conscious breathing also affects public speaking performance.

As we saw in the last chapter, breathing—especially the exhaled breath—can significantly reduce the physical stress responses associated with speech anxiety. Now let's talk about how focused breath makes you a stronger speaker. If you think that I'm referring to vocal production and power, you're right. But equally important is the emotional connection you have to your material and audience. Perhaps best of all, knowing how to use your breath helps make you aware and *present*.

As Kathy Lubar and Belle Halpern—stage performers and co-authors of the book *Leadership Presence*—put it: "You can't avoid being in the present, if you concentrate on your breath."[3] It turns out that breathing consciously is a key aspect of speaking with presence. Your new focus on the conscious, controlled breath will make you more aware and present—in a word, more "mindful" of this moment.

As soon as you develop that level of mindfulness, you become more present for your listeners. That also means being more fully responsive to the moment at hand, and better able to think on your feet. The more high-stakes your speech or presentation, the more you require that last ability. You need it to answer questions and to deal with unforeseen challenges and pushback. More generally, it helps you to become completely aware of the moment-by-moment exchange that should take place between you and an audience.

You can understand from this discussion why the ability to speak with presence is an integral part of peak performance.

But how in practical terms does breathing help you to make a connection with your audience? After all, people can't see your breath. We've already discussed one way in the last chapter: mindful breathing takes your attention off the physical distress that can preoccupy you if you have speech anxiety. There are also two other ways that conscious breathing contributes to greater skill and focus on your part. The first has to do with the link between breath and voice; and the second, with strengthening your own emotional connection to your content.

BREATHING AND VOCAL ENERGY

In a sense, your breath is the opening phase of vocal production. That's because it is the raw material for activating the vocal folds (technically the thyroarytenoid muscles) in your larynx that produce vocal sound. The production of your voice is a three-phase process: First, air pressure moves toward the vocal folds. Second, exhaled air moves upward toward them through movement of the diaphragm and muscles in the abdomen, chest, and rib cage. Third, the vocal folds vibrate as the bottom of the folds and then the top close, releasing a pulse of air. This cycle is repeated. The air pulses create a buzzing sound, which is then amplified by the resonators in the body.[4] We recognize the result of these finely orchestrated movements and release of energy as the human voice.

Note how the first two of the three phases—air pressure and exhalation—depend by definition upon air or breath. What matters for anyone desiring greater stage presence, is *how you use this vocal energy to reach listeners*. You're not just making vocal sounds which would just be grunting! It's the amazing confluence of thought, breath, and intention, transformed into the power of what you actually say that becomes speech.

The voice, then (and therefore thoughts expressed aloud) starts with the breath! Ask yourself this: What could be more intimate than something that comes from inside your body that you use to connect with the thoughts of others?[5] Once you grasp this idea, you can understand how closely breathing is aligned with how you express yourself.

And here's a wonderful thought from the world of spoken drama: "We have to make the breath and the muscular formation of the words *the means by which the thought is released*."[6] Of course! Apart from body language, there is no other way for the thought to be released in spoken performance. You can see, then, how important it is to connect your breath—the energy with which you speak—to the words.

In the next chapter on the voice, I'll discuss how that is done. For now—since we've seen how your breathing is linked to vocal production and energy—let's talk about how good breathing connects you emotionally with your material. Once you've achieved that link, it's much easier to get anything you believe in across to your audience.

THE EMOTIONAL AND PHYSICAL CONNECTION

At this point, you've learned that exhalation is far more than just stale air—it's an essential part of the channeling of energy that makes your voice possible. Apart from activating the vocal folds, your exhalation is also the key to *supporting* the sound you're making—in other words, providing enough breath so that all of your words are heard.

There are two important reasons why this is so. The first is that unlike passive or vegetative breathing, when you speak, *you must increase the duration of the exhalation and begin to control it.* For instance, try explaining aloud a complex idea while exhaling passively, the way you do when you're sitting quietly reading a book. You'll find that you can't do it. Saying anything more than a couple of words requires a sustained exhalation, since it's continually exhaled air that powers the vocal fold cycles necessary for prolonged speech.

The other reason you need a longer exhalation when you speak is that in English, the most important idea is usually expressed at the end of the thought. For example, take what it perhaps the most famous quote in our language: Hamlet said, "To be or not to be, that is the QUESTION." He didn't say, "The QUESTION is whether to be or not to be." Can you hear how much weaker that second construction is? Very often, what we are saying needs to be punched at the end, because that is the culmination of the thought. Obviously, you need to sustain the exhalation for long enough that you don't run out of vocal energy at this important moment!

Sustaining your exhalation, then, is central to keeping you in control. By 'control,' I mean a result that (1) calms you (as we saw in the last chapter on overcoming speaking fear by activating the vagus nerve); (2) projects your sound sufficiently to where the audience is situated; and (3) uses phrasing and pacing to make your main points crystal clear.

Concerning that last item, consider this comparison: *You* know how the parts of your speech fit together and how logic and language help you prove your point. You should also be aware of where the climax comes and where you make your strongest case. But if it all rolls out without any pacing, pauses, or moments for the drama to build, your audience will miss out on what you're really trying to accomplish. Using breathing to help control your pace (including pauses) will help your spoken performance reach another level of interest and "listenability" for your audience. Undifferentiated vocal delivery never achieves that. And of course, always remember that extraordinary speakers *perform* their speeches not just spit out content!

Equally important is your emotional connection to your material; and this too depends partly on your use of breath. Your new awareness of the conscious controlled breath automatically makes you more aware and present—more mindful of this moment and place. This has unlimited value in making you more present for your listeners and able to respond to their needs (and even their challenges). When you're connected to your own emotions as well as those of your listeners, you automatically come across as more of a leader.

Breathing and the Present Moment

Being in the present moment is nowhere more necessary than when you're speaking to hundreds or thousands of people. Here in particular, conscious breathing is an essential tool in your arsenal.

This need for mindfulness and presence clashes with one of the biggest challenges of the 21st century: the increasing distortion of our sense of time. Being constantly online; the mind-jarring shifts in our attention due to multitasking; ever-multiplying social media channels; the never-ending barrage of advertising and marketing messages; and our shrinking attention spans due to TV shows, commercials, and movies that substitute speed and frantic action for meaning...each of these phenomena change how we experience time. (Did you, in fact, become impatient with that last intentionally complex sentence?)

These continual demands on our brain and nervous system lead to what Dennis Lewis describes as "a low-grade but chronic fight or flight or freeze state, in which...the constant release of adrenaline and cortisol undermines our immune system and throws us into increasingly negative states of disharmony."[7]

The danger, of course, is that this stressed-out state becomes our norm—that we consider it a *necessary* response to our environment. Here's a personal story about how mindful breathing can help shield you against a stressed-out feeling of "fast-forward all the time."

For some years, I've attended an annual conference sponsored by one of my clients, a Boston-based healthcare organization. A few years ago, while strolling through the tradeshow hall during a break in speakers, I decided to participate in a demonstration of a vendor's product. This product is a band worn around the head that measures electrical brain signals. The device is meant to train users in employing biofeedback to achieve a calmer and more serene state of mind.

Here's how the product works: while wearing the band, you listen through headphones to a sound stimulus for three minutes—the choice was a thunderstorm or ocean waves crashing. (I chose the stormy weather.) Your job as wearer of the device is to try to quiet the thunder or crashing waves you're hearing. If your brainwaves as measured by the device reflect scattered or chaotic thinking, the sound will become louder. Conversely, if your thoughts (vis-a-vis your brain's electrical activity) are calm, the thunder or waves will decrease in volume. By learning to use biofeedback, you'll soon be able to become calmer and more focused.

There I was, then, flying through a storm (you might say). I didn't appear to be too close to it, however, because I only heard very faint thunder. So, to make things more interesting, I tried to make my thoughts agitated. My reward was a barely-audible blip in the rumble from that distant storm.

When my test drive was over, the technician recorded the results. He told me my score was 93. Not knowing if that was good or horrible, I asked how most people scored. I wanted to know if I was good at bio-feedback, or a pitiful specimen of humanity.

"You meditate, right?" was the technician's answer.

"No."

"C'mon, you meditate," he insisted. "Nobody gets a 93 on their first try!"

I assured him that I didn't practice meditation (though I've tried it from time to time). But I mentioned that I use mindful breathing on a daily basis, and have done so as a stage actor for many decades. In fact, I said, I teach the techniques as a speech coach, trainer, author, and key-note speaker.

He shared with me that one of the Dalai Lama's assistants—a person who teaches meditation—had scored a 95 when he tried the device. I wondered, however, if he was just flattering me to make a sale. So, later that day, I asked a friend I've known for years who was also attending the conference if he had tried the device. "Sure," he said. "Let's see...I think I scored somewhere in the 40s."

That's when I realized just how strongly controlled and mindful breathing can help shape your response to the environment you find yourself in.

Breath and Language

Finally, let's consider how the breath as part of the physical expression of what you're saying aids you as a communicator. The breath, in

fact, "takes the words down to a physical level, deeper than the intellect... [where] passion is allowed to come through the language, with its
enormous variety of sounds."[8]

Breath then is connected not just to vocalization but also to *language itself*. One of the things acting teaches you—especially if it's in
Shakespeare's plays—is to trust in the language. We can apply that concept directly to public speaking as well, and say this:

If you trust in what you're saying, all you have to do is say it.

You don't have to be a monumental performer who bestrides the
world like a Colossus (yep, that's Shakespeare). You *do* have to breathe:
fully and from the diaphragm, because that's the source of the power
that gives your words life. If you're breathing shallowly now, you need
to *lower* the breath in your body. Remember, that's where your power
comes from—not from the chest area, and certainly not from your
throat. Breathe with your diaphragm and you'll be in touch with the
core process that produces vocal sound. As I said earlier, speech begins
with the breath! Get in touch with your breathing as you speak and
you'll begin to *own* the words you're uttering.

Avoid a "Head Voice." The cerebral or "head voice" that so many
people use, on the other hand, results from much shallower breathing.
A voice like that reveals not only an over-emphasis on thinking (rather
than feeling and displaying emotion), but also neglecting the body in
performance. When this is the speaking style, that person literally has
to learn how to sink the voice so it resonates in the rest of the body not
just the head.

When you link your breathing to how you express yourself physically, you're tapping into a strong emotional response. You are also discovering how to convey emotions powerfully to others. Often, it is at
that point that you begin to understand your own feelings! That is why
breathing exercises in classes and theatrical rehearsals sometimes bring
people to tears. We will learn more about this connection between voice,
emotions, and full expression in the next chapter.

CHAPTER 6

Vocal Dynamics: Transforming Your Relationship with Your Audience

The voice will ring as passion strikes its chords. [It] is the intermediary between ourselves and our hearers, [and] will produce precisely the same emotion in the judge that we have put into it. For it is the index of the mind, and is capable of expressing all its variety of feelings.

—Quintilian

Don't look at me, sir, with—ah—in that tone of voice.

—Punch

Welcome to the wonder of your voice! It's your most powerful public speaking performance tool for persuading, inspiring, and moving audiences. If you get to be a memorable speaker, one reason will most likely be because of your voice. We talk about the figurative "voice" as the voice of a generation, the voice of leadership, etc. But your actual physical voice, more than any other performance technique, reflects who you are when you speak to others. Equally important: it's your instrument par excellence for *eliciting in others the same emotions you are feeling.*

To speak with impact and influence, you must acquire the tools of full vocal expressiveness. I learned this lesson firsthand at the Webber Douglas Academy of Dramatic Art in London, where I completed my actor training. There, and at the other British acting academies, students work diligently on the technical aspects of vocal production. They do so to achieve the freedom and power that comes from training one's instrument and knowing how to use it. The human voice differs from other instruments in that you can train *it*, not merely train yourself to play it.

What Your Voice Reveals

Often, you will find that when your voice is not performing the way you want it to, the fault will be related in some way to your own intentions being out of balance. For instance, if your voice sounds tight and tense as you're advocating a point of view, that is probably because you're straining too hard for the end result of persuasion, rather than taking the time to build your case logically. If you believe you have solid evidence to support your argument, why would you become strident?

Cicely Berry gives us some marvelous examples of the connection between mental and emotional states and how the voice reveals them. Consider the following:

> Diction not clear = Not being precise enough in thought or not carrying the thought all the way through to the words.

> Trailing away at the end of phrases = Not thinking through to the end of a thought.

> Stiff jaw and immovable lips = Reluctance to communicate.[1]

Do you see how the way you express yourself vocally is closely linked to your thinking and motives? Your voice is thus an excellent barometer of how simply and honestly you are getting across to people. Part of your success then depends upon your ability to express yourself physically. That means through body language, certainly, but also voice. It all has to do with drawing the audience in to truly listen.

BREATHING AND FREEING THE VOICE

In order to allow your voice to reflect your thoughts and feelings—and to help you physically express what you mean to say—you have to free it. As we've seen, vocal production starts with breathing as air pressure and exhaled breath excite the vocal folds, which then produce sound. So, to release your voice fully, you first must free your breath.

Remember the "head voice" which I mentioned that so many people use nowadays? Scottish voice coach Kristin Linklater characterizes that situation as splitting yourself in two, with one part of you speaking, and the other part observing from above and commenting on your own performance.[2] Obviously, such speakers don't trust their vocal production enough to let it freely express what they're thinking and feeling.

In the last chapter, you learned that your breath is fundamental to the essence of who you are—that you and your breathing are the same. Consequently, when your breath is released without obstruction, *you* are released. In this sense, your listeners receive much more than the simple sounds coming from your mouth. They hear the "unobstructed you"—the free flow of your thoughts and emotions. What could be more intimate than to share the breath that flows from inside you and results in your authentic voice?

You can see how your breath and voice are responsible for much of your performance. And since the voice uses the body to express itself, you must master physical performance to gain control over your vocal instrument. There's no way around it: your voice is produced physically. How incredible that that fact is often overlooked![3]

VOICE AND POWER

Knowing this, your task now becomes not only creating a voice that gets your message across. It must also be strong enough—powerful enough—to create absolute confidence in you and what you say.

To develop such a strong voice, you start (as we've seen) with breath. A voice created through good diaphragmatic breathing literally embodies strength and power. But it also projects the type of resonance that's both authoritative and pleasant to listen to. That combination is a recipe for literally achieving "the sound of leadership."

Try the following experiment to convince yourself of this truth. Stand up, and imagine you're in a large conference room with twenty to thirty people. Exhale *almost* all of the air from your lungs. Say to the group, "Hi everyone. I'm your leader, and I want you to follow me." (Never mind whether this scenario is realistic!) Now fill up your lungs, and repeat the same words out loud.... Which version of you in fact sounds like a leader?

I'll wager that you could immediately hear the difference in terms of the fullness, strength, and authority of your vocal sound. For one thing, you can't adequately project your voice if you have no air to do it with—remember it is exhaled air that activates the vocal folds. That means that a voice unsupported by sufficient breath is weak and doesn't carry very far.

It is also deficient in terms of quality and resonance, and even affects your appearance. I'll bet that in the first part of the exercise above, your upper body assumed a slightly concave posture when you expelled nearly all the air from your lungs. Insufficient breathing can affect even your body language, then, so that you *look* less like a leader!

To recap: creating a fuller sound means starting the process in the belly area, not the throat. The way you produce more vocal power is by pulling the diaphragm inwards as you exhale. This propels the air upwards, applying more force to the exhaled air to activate the vocal folds. Most of the time we're not conscious of this process; and we may even try to make our voices louder by tightening (and straining) the vocal cords. But it's in the belly not the throat where well-supported sound begins!

To feel this in action, imagine that you're trying to get the attention of someone far away from you. Place your hand on your belly and say, "*Hey!*" loudly enough to get their attention. Did you feel how strongly you contracted the diaphragm to produce a voice that would carry farther?

Using the voice in this way is also important in terms of vocal health. If, as I mentioned above, you attempt to make your voice louder by tightening your vocal cords, the sound will increase in volume. But your voice will almost certainly become harsher and unpleasant. Equally bad, you'll be straining and irritating the muscles of the larynx. That's why a couple of hours of shouting over the band at a rock concert or the music at a loud club will leave you hoarse. Your vocal folds will start to heal once you stop the shouting and get some rest. But abusing your voice like this over time—as some pop singers have been finding out lately—can lead to serious problems. That can lead to surgery to remove vocal nodules, or hard noncancerous growths that are like built-up calluses from too much friction on these delicate muscles of the larynx.

Sustaining the Sound (and the Thought)

What about the link between sound and sense that I mentioned earlier? Producing a strong voice won't be very helpful if you don't *sustain* it through the end of your thought. A common problem of speakers, in fact, is allowing an important point or idea to trail off at the end because their voice fades away. Yet most of the time in spoken English, the end of the phrase is where the payoff comes. Remember that while we write in sentences, we speak in ideas. That's one reason why spoken language generally uses shorter expressions than written concepts that can be worked out in whole paragraphs. In order to make your point, keep your voice "supported" by breath until you finish the thought. If you express that idea briefly enough for maximum impact, so much the better!

Fortunately, it's not hard to learn to speak this way. It's a simple two-step process: (1) 'Belly breathe' to give yourself good breath capacity; then (2) support the sound to the end of the idea, i.e., don't let your voice trail off. Tape yourself and listen back—you'll immediately hear whether your voice is both strong and stays so to the end of each thought.

VOCAL DYNAMICS

Let's say you've accomplished the steps described above. You've freed the voice through diaphragmatic breathing; and by doing so you've created a reservoir of air for a healthy and powerful sound. Congratulations! Now it's time to discuss vocal expressiveness or what I call *vocal dynamics*.

As speakers we all naturally focus on the content of our presentations—the things we're going to say. But content is only one channel of communication. There's an equally important and productive channel in terms of dynamic stage presence: our vocal expressiveness.

Where Are *You*...and Why Should People Listen? The use of the full palette of vocal coloration is one of your most vital means of reaching and moving people, because it brings your personality into what you're saying. Remember, you are trying to persuade your audience to think, feel, or *do* what you want them to!

For example, you can discuss last quarter's earnings or the company's new product line, and that's fine. But where are *you*? If you allow your true voice to be heard, you can invest your topics with your own response to the information, and that's vital for the speaker-audience dynamic to click. Doing this usually means employing more of the range that your voice is capable of. Your voice helps get your message across because people hear you, not just the data. It's all part of getting your meaning across and convincing listeners of why they need to hear it. This in fact is a mandate of all the speaking you do.

Sounding Like You Mean It

You've heard the truism before: *how* you say what you say matters as much as the words themselves.

For instance, you can answer the question: "Do you love me?" with a curt, "Yes." (Scrolling through messages on your cellphone while you reply is optional.) Or you can pour feeling into that small word: "*Yeeees*"…so that it *sounds* like, "Oh, you have no idea how much!"

In the curt response, your significant other would most likely hear, "Yeah, a little." In the second example, however, he or she hears genuine feeling. And in the quality of how you express that single small word is a validation of the entire relationship (or not). All through a one-syllable response! Clearly, *the meaning of what you intend to convey depends directly on your ability to use your voice to express it.*

Let's see this in action in the context of a slightly longer expression (what we would call a *sentence* if we were writing it). Say the phrase given below out loud. Actually, you'll be speaking it six times, emphasizing a different word each time. Typically, we emphasize words by raising both our volume and pitch, and you can do that here.

You'll be speaking the phrase out loud six times, then. The first time you'll raise the volume and inflect your voice on the first word "I"; next, you'll do so only on the second word "didn't;" the third time on "give," and so on. Record yourself if you like.

"I didn't give them those documents."

What you just communicated aloud was: (1) "I didn't give them those documents"; (2) "I DIDN'T give them those documents"; (3) "I didn't GIVE them those documents"; (4) "I didn't give THEM those documents"; (5) "I didn't give them THOSE documents"; and (6) "I didn't give them those DOCUMENTS."

You've just conveyed six different messages! Do you see how the way you use your voice invests words with meaning? Perhaps you can understand now that any speaker who blandly reads from notes or slides is leaving out at least 50 percent of what he wants to convey to an audience.

This skill is particularly vital when it comes to conveying the emotional content of a speech. In fact, it's nearly impossible to do so unless you enlist the help of vocal dynamics. So, take this important fact to heart:

**Your greatest tool for persuading listeners
is the way you use your voice.**

There isn't another component of a presentation that's capable of such infinite variety. And only this tool in your performance toolbox can achieve such subtle shades of meaning and intention. Think about that: how often have you understood what a speaker really meant by the way she said the words?

When it comes to your own career, invest some time in discovering how effectively you can use your voice. Record yourself and listen to the intentions and feelings embodied in your sound. Try to grasp (or ask others) how people are hearing you then make any necessary decisions about how you need to improve. You may find that people think you have certain attitudes, or that you come across in ways very different from what you intended. As always, practice out loud so you can hear any changes or progress!

The Magic of Your Voice: Part of the magic of using the voice effectively is that *it should elicit in listeners the same response you have toward what you are saying*. Nothing else in your performance repertoire allows that to happen so reliably, unless it's a particularly powerful visual image. And then, of course, what you say about that image will help lead audiences toward *feeling* about it the way you want them to.

The Emotional Connection

Now let's spend some time on that all-important emotional response in others. In particular, let's look at how the emotion in your voice can light up the same feeling in your audience. When listeners hear emotion in your voice, their human response means that they experience the same emotion themselves. That's because of "mirror neurons" in the brain that allow each of us to respond as fellow members of the same species.

Your ability to express outwardly what you feel, then, is a huge factor in developing leadership presence in public speaking. And it's undoubtedly more important in business and professional speaking than most people realize. Being too "businesslike" and serious when speaking is a risky approach than can leave out the entire emotional spectrum. And audiences are operating within that spectrum all the time, whether they know it or not. They're responding to it as they accept, reject, or remain indifferent to what you say, and make decisions concerning what they should do as a result of it. Just as important, it's helping them to decide who and what *you* are, and whether you're a credible conveyor of your message.

We know this is true because brain researchers have been aware for some time that *all* decisions—including those in business, politics, personal relationships, and everything else—involve an emotional component. If you aren't able to use full vocal expressiveness, you'll leave out emotional clues, nuances, and modeling that help audiences decide in favor of you and your ideas.

Actor Danny Kaye once said, "All that matters is what you feel when you say the words."[4] That is not quite true—but nearly so. Everyone gets better at communicating when they allow how they feel about something to show. It brings an "aliveness, vigor, and conviction" to the proceedings.[5] We can even understand how emotions are imbued in the voice in evolutionary terms. As Berry puts it, "It is quite probable that linguistically we made open sounds before we made closed ones; and that therefore the vowel carries our instinctive, primitive meanings."[6]

The Painting Analogy

Here's an analogy I use to get clients to understand how important it is to bring emotions into their speech. Think of a painting that you particularly enjoyed while visiting a museum. The painting itself, of course, elicited your emotional response. But where did the picture begin and end, i.e., how was it displayed so that you could experience it? It was the *picture frame* that allowed that to happen, by supplying the painting's boundaries: that is, where the painting ended and the wall began!

To translate that into public speaking terms: When you speak emotionally, it's mostly the vowels of the words you use that convey your feelings ("love," "dr*ea*m" "*a*mazing"), while consonants tell listeners where syllables and words begin and end. To use the museum metaphor: the emotional content of your voice (expressed through vowels) is the painting; and the consonants that you speak "frame" the emotion-expressing vowels by allowing them to be heard as words and ideas. Without that framing effect, you'd only be uttering emotional sounds without anything to shape them into language.

Improving Your Business Speaking. Do you grasp why allowing your emotions to live through open vowel sounds will bring life and passion to your voice? Just as the painting is the soul of the artist's work, the sounds you convey clue listeners in to the essence of what you *feel* about what you're saying. How can you accomplish this in practice? By avoiding the clipped "businesslike" delivery that's so common, and that completely leaves out the emotional connection. In other words, linger for longer on the vowel sounds, because they are there for a reason. Even a brief statement such as "The results were amazing," said blandly and without expression can't compete with "The results were am*aaa*zing!" You can understand why so much business speech lacks a beating heart.

You needn't worry that you must spend time picking out the vowels in the words you say. As you put together an idea then express it aloud, the language you're using is already helping you reach listeners on an intellectual *and* emotional basis. In fact, you chose those words because they help you express a thought or idea. All you really need to do in practice is *invest* yourself in them. Simply become more alive to the language you're using. The more your voice can tap into the power of the words *you have chosen*, the more life and meaning those words will have for your audience.

One last admonition: just be sure to earn the emotions you're conveying. In other words, don't aim for a cheap effect by trying to manipulate your audience into feeling something. That's the domain of advertisers, con artists, and even some moviemakers who are only interested in extracting money out of people's wallets.

Rather than going down the manipulation road, share your emotional response as you really feel it. Audiences will hear that emotion and respond to it more reliably than almost any other technique you can employ in speaking.

You're aware now of how vowel sounds carry essential emotional meaning. How else can you achieve full voice expressiveness or *vocal dynamics?* That's what the close-up below is all about. I call it "The 5 Key Tools of Vocal Dynamics."

CLOSE-UP

The 5 Key Tools of Vocal Dynamics

There are many advantages to having a lively and expressive voice. They include speaking with more impact and power. Qualities such as warmth, authority, empathy, trustworthiness, passion, intelligence, assertiveness, and many others are only revealed when a speaker uses the full "color palette" of the voice. If you can achieve vocal dynamics, you will dramatically improve your ability to engage and influence listeners.

To accomplish this, you need to be familiar with five essential vocal tools:

1. **Energy and emphasis**
2. **Pitch inflection**
3. **Variety in rhythm and pace**
4. **Pauses and silence**
5. **Vocal quality**

Let's look at each of them in turn.

1. **Energy and emphasis** concern the *force or stress* you place on important ideas, concepts, or feelings. Doing so means you have an energized vocal style. It is the simplest of the 5 essential vocal tools and you probably already use it well. Be aware, however, that speeches and presentations are performances; and that any form of performance requires a level of energy above the ordinary.

2. **Pitch inflection** refers to raising and lowering your pitch on the musical scale. It has to do with the frequency, i.e., speed of vibration at which you speak. Sometimes called *intonation*, lively pitch inflection helps you avoid monotony as well as convey meaning.

Many speakers use a too-narrow pitch range, limiting their voice's natural ability to express emotion. If you find that your voice is "flat" when speaking professionally, listen to how you sound when you're with people you're comfortable around. You probably use much livelier pitch inflection on those occasions because you're not self-conscious and "trying." Invite *that* person to speak at your next presentation!

3. Your **rhythm and pace** also need to be varied so your audience stays attentive and aware of any nuances in your speech. But don't try to plan ahead of time where you will alter the pace. If you *invest* yourself fully in what you're saying (as I mentioned above in terms of vowel sounds and emotions), the pace will vary naturally as your ideas and emotions change from moment to moment. You can easily tell when speakers aren't invested emotionally in what they are saying because their performances have a metronomic quality.

4. **Pauses and silence** is a tool you may be neglecting, because many of us don't trust silence! Pauses in a speech are valuable, however, for a number of reasons. They can add emphasis, build suspense, bridge ideas, make a comment on what you just said, and most important, allow enough time for important points to sink in. They also give your audience the chance to take a mental breath and "hit the reset button" in their brains. In addition, anxious speakers are at the mercy of too much adrenaline in their bloodstream, which speeds everything up, including their speech. That typically banishes *any* pauses, and can make an audience feel exhausted just listening. If that's you, go back to the section in Chapter 4 labeled "Breathing to Calm and Relax Yourself" to get back on an even keel.

5. **Vocal quality** is the most all-encompassing of the 5 vocal tools. It includes the tone of your voice and its richness and pleasantness. Other factors associated with vocal quality include breathiness, tentativeness, tension, warmth vs. stridency, patience vs. impatience, empathy vs. indifference, and other impressions that affect people's emotional response and confidence in you. No wonder it's the most inclusive of the essential tools!

You might change your vocal quality, for instance, when you want to lead your audience to a certain emotional response—such as a whispered phrase to evoke mystery or intimacy. Employing different vocal qualities throughout a talk is part of what makes you an interesting speaker.

The key to the 5 essential vocal tools is that they should be used *together* rather than in isolation. Now that you know what they are, employ them all, because they are at your disposal anytime. Your audiences will stay tuned more readily, pay closer attention to what you're saying, and be more easily moved and persuaded.

THE VOICE AND LANGUAGE

In the final section of this chapter, I'll share with you how to improve your impact on audiences while simultaneously making your performances memorable. I'm talking about using your voice to reflect the beauty and power of language.

Spoken words consist of sounds, of course. Yet, in a way few of us realize, the sound of words is related to their sense. I don't only mean words that embody the well-known 'onomatopoeia,' or those that sound like what they mean, such as "hiss," "splat," "woe," or "tap." I mean the relationships of words to each other, and how the vowel and consonant sounds you employ give us hints as to your emotions and intentions. Another way to explain the connection to sound and sense is that the human voice invokes responses in a way that no other stimuli can accomplish.

As the great theater director Peter Brook put it in referring to spoken verse (a heightened form of language): "Good verse strikes echoes in the speaker that awaken portions of his deep experience which are seldom evoked in everyday speech."[7] That is, spoken words marry sound and sense for all to hear. They impact listeners in a way that's simply not possible when those same words are read silently.

Clearly, then, there's a relationship between the physical and the emotional. And that means *you need to use both to move listeners.* Only in performance will your speech or presentation reach its full potential in terms of affecting an audience. You therefore must be aware of the sounds your words are making, because they are revealing part of their sense! Let me give an example:

In Shakespeare's play *Macbeth*, the title character, a nobleman and military leader, is contemplating assassinating King Duncan and seizing the throne. As he argues with himself, we hear his thinking in the *soliloquy* he says out loud. Here is the first line-and-a-half of his speech:

"If it were done when 'tis done, then 'twere well
It were done quickly."

Here Macbeth is trying to come to grips with whether killing the king and seizing his throne, i.e., gaining worldly power, is worth eternal damnation. In modern language: "If it would be all over with the killing, then I may as well do it quickly." (A few lines later in this speech he refers to *"The deep damnation of his taking-off."*)

Notice how the first lines I've quoted reflect this idea that immediate gain—to be accomplished quickly—must be measured against eternal judgment. The word "done," spoken three times in fourteen words contains a long vowel sound. (So does the word "well".) These long sounds literally stretch the spoken line in time, reminding us of eternity. But the argument Macbeth is making here is in *favor* of killing King Duncan—so the thought ends with: "*quickly.*" You can hear the almost exquisite juxtaposition of the long-vowel of "done" juxtaposed with the *two* short-vowel sounds in "quickly": "kw ick li" (the short "i" sound). Thus, Macbeth ends this reflection on long-lasting punishment with a thought (expressed in the word he's chosen) that if he can get it over with *quickly* perhaps all will be well. In the end, this is exactly what he decides; and he stabs Duncan to death while the king is sleeping.

You can hear, even in this brief excerpt from one of Shakespeare's soliloquies, how the sound of well-chosen words reflects their meaning in terms of what the audience understands. Emotions and sense come through, not only sheer information. You can also see that the words Shakespeare uses (aside from 'tis and 'twere' which are easily understood when spoken) are the same ones you and I might use, i.e., this relationship of word-sounds and meaning hasn't changed at all from his era to ours.

Making Your Words Impactful. Fortunately, you don't have to agonize over your choice of words for sound-sense as you're putting your presentation together. Your knowledge of your topic and your intuition about what you're saying will allow that to happen subconsciously. On the other hand, it's the perfect reason you should be practicing your talk out loud. *You* need to hear if your words reflect the intention behind what you're saying (through their sound as well as their meaning) before your audience does! Practicing out loud is also the perfect opportunity to change your choice of words if other choices sound more accurate or impactful.

Voice Meets Text: More on Sound and Meaning

In the 1940s through 1960s, Hollywood began to comment on its own lavish period of earlier horror films by producing what I call the "Meet" movies. These were often tongue-and-cheek offerings that satirized the studios' own earlier efforts. They included such deathless classics as *Dracula Meets the Wolfman* (1943), *Abbott and Costello Meet the Mummy* (1955), and *Jesse James Meets Frankenstein's Daughter* (1966…including this immortal marketing copy: "Roaring guns against raging monster!"). As you may gather from the titles, these movies were mostly for fun and didn't always take themselves seriously.

How do you tap into the magic of language this way in your own speeches, lectures, presentations, and remarks? Well, you start with the earlier sections of this chapter on understanding and using the five essential vocal tools. Then you go one big step beyond that requirement, by investing your words with what we might call "the full sound of commitment." You know which phrases or ideas demand this type of response from you so that everyone knows what you're really getting at. It's just a matter of putting it into operation.

Your voice "meets" the text of your remarks in a similar way when you speak in public. Let's say you've subconsciously chosen language (as I just explained) that will work effectively in terms of delivering your message to this audience. When you're actually speaking—right at that point—your voice exists to make that material come to life. There are no speech tricks involved. It's simply a case of literally *embodying* the voice.

As Royal Shakespeare Company director John Barton says, "You must make the words "fresh-minted" as you say them, as if you've just invented them!"[8] This is easier to do than you might think at first. Simply pour the meaning you intend into the way you express what you're saying. Don't hold back: *commit yourself*. What Barton means is that if you imbue the word or phrase with the full sense of how you intend it, it will sound brand-new and filled with meaning to your listeners. And of course, the emotional component will be strongly present. Contrast that with presenters who drone on through their presentations with no emotional involvement whatsoever.

Audiences need to experience your commitment and dynamism through your physical performance! If they don't, they will be struck by the disconnect: "Why is she so monotone if all of this is as urgent as she says it is?" "He says he's 100% behind this idea, but he doesn't sound like it." Some of my clients are CFOs, and believe me, financial analysts pay close attention in earnings calls to whether these executives sound committed to their upbeat projections. The truth is that if you invest yourself—mentally, emotionally, and physically—in your message as you deliver it, you can transform your experience with an audience, including their relationship with you.

Let's talk more about the art of physical expression. That's the topic of the next chapter.

WORDS AND MUSIC

Mark Twain was famous as a speaker as well as a humorist. One morning as he was getting dressed, he discovered that a button was missing from his shirt. He was annoyed, and reached for another shirt. But that one was missing a button as well. He tried a third time…and discovered yet *another* missing button!

Furious, he began swearing loudly, like the miner he once was. After he had finished, he looked up to see his wife in the doorway, scowling at him because of his intemperance. Slowly and emotionlessly, she repeated every obscenity that her husband had just used.

The task took a while. When she had finished, she stood there in silence, trusting that her recital had shamed the great writer. Instead, with a gleam in his eye, Twain puffed on his cigar and said, "My dear, you have the words, but you don't have the music."[9]

CHAPTER 7

Body Language:
The Art of Physical Expression

Your words need to take up dwelling in your listeners. How is that
going to happen if you don't *embody* them? What you do with your
audience is more dance than conversation.

—*Jana Childers*

No mortal can keep a secret. If his lips are silent, he chatters
with his fingertips; betrayal oozes out of him at every pore.

—*Sigmund Freud*

You want to *move* your listeners, don't you? That means you have to move.

Like an actor in rehearsal trying to connect with the action of the
play, you should literally move when you speak in public to help create
a visual component to the forward momentum of your ideas. Your body
is one of your key means of communication; and if you don't employ
it, you diminish the strength and impact of your presentation. You also
make it more difficult for yourself to show what you feel. As audiences,
we depend upon that visual demonstration to *see* that you're committed
and passionate about what you say you believe.

ARE YOU INTERESTING TO WATCH WHEN YOU SPEAK?

Do you know why some salespeople keep a mirror by their telephone at
work? It's because they know that their facial expressions can be "heard"
on the other end. These people are often taught to smile before they pick

up the receiver (or click the "Answer" prompt on their cell phone), so that they will sound friendly when they say hello. It's just one example of how what you do physically is reflected in people's responses to you.

When I'm working with a client on using body language, I often suggest that they practice in front of a mirror. I tell them to give their talk exactly as they will when it's time to perform the speech—including forming all the words—but without vocalizing. In another words, they should *look* exactly as they will in performance, including movement, gestures, and facial expressions, though it will all be delivered in silence. Then, I suggest, they should ask themselves some questions:

- "Am I an interesting speaker to watch, apart from what I'm saying?"
- "Do I have an animated presence...or am I too statue-like?"
- "Can people tell how I feel about this topic just by looking at me?"
- "Do I display enough passion to back up my ideas?"
- "Do I appear to be reaching out to the audience to connect with them?"

The Physical Dimension to Your Speech. All of these questions touch upon a *physical dimension* to your public speaking. Audiences depend upon your eye contact, facial expressions, gestures, stance, posture, movement on stage, and generally, a "reaching out" to them. You should never plan out your gestures or facial expressions. But you should be aware that you *have* a physical presence and not just get up there and deliver information while remaining as wooden as the lectern.

Speaking to groups is an opportunity (of course!) to connect with others who share your interest and passion for a subject. And your nonverbal expressiveness is an indispensable part of the exchange.

JUST HOW IMPORTANT IS BODY LANGUAGE?

We're told that nonverbal behaviors constitute 60 to 65 percent of interpersonal communication.[1] Another famous study claimed that the number can be as high as 93 percent, at least when discussing feelings or attitudes.[2] And one well-known researcher claims that at least 90 percent of emotional messages are nonverbal.[3]

With numbers like these, it's hard to dispute that a strong undercurrent of audience response depends upon what you display as a speaker.

In other words, a large part of your influence depends upon what you are showing, not just what you're saying. It's the old idea that "it isn't what you say, but how you say it." Among the tools for speaking memorably include the vocal dynamics I discussed in the last chapter. But another equally powerful one is your ability to incorporate *physical expressiveness*.

Lessons From a TED Talk. You can see this in action in what is currently the seventh most popular TED Talk: Jill Bolte Taylor's "My Stroke of Insight." The title of the talk is a clever play on words because Dr. Taylor—herself a brain scientist—suffered a massive stroke in 1996 at the age of thirty-seven, requiring an eight-year recovery.[4] Dr. Taylor's talk is fascinating because of her unique viewpoint and experience. That is, she both experienced and observed the deterioration of her brain's language and cognitive abilities over a four-hour period after a blood vessel "exploded."

Apart from her remarkable recovery—demonstrated by her incisive and fascinating speech—her TED Talk is a lesson in how to translate one's spoken content into the physical expression of that material. Dr. Taylor is particularly effective at using her arms and hands expansively in a way that reflects the size and scope of her topic. If you watch the talk, you'll also notice how she moves within the tight red circle (the hallmark of TED Talks), while pivoting regularly to display her upper body to every part of the audience. Here's a speaker who understands the need to move while speaking on the public stage!

Presenters who move are certainly more interesting to watch than those who are "talking heads." But learning to use body language while speaking actually involves a more fundamental issue. It's this: physical expression—along with other forms of nonverbal communication—has the power to transcend cognitive thinking. For one thing, it's capable of producing a *gestalt* or wholesale comprehension of a concept without a complex thinking process leading to a conclusion. Such forms of expression can be very powerful, even explosive "Aha!" moments. One way they can be generated is through a presentation that's literally *embodied* by the speaker.

So, pay attention to the care and feeding of the physical aspects of your speaking persona. If you haven't ever thought that you need to express yourself physically as well as intellectually in a presentation,

I hope this chapter convinces you. As modern dance pioneer Martha Graham put it, "The body says what words cannot."[5]

Once again, then, the question: how important is body language? In law enforcement, appropriate body language can be a matter of life or death. In an FBI study of criminals who had attacked police officers, the prisoners revealed that they scoped out how easy a target an officer would be based on such factors as sloppy or neat dress, and how he or she carried themselves. (Vague and imprecise language when dealing with suspects was also considered.) The conclusion?—In approaching a suspect, "poor vocal tone and body language could get you killed."[6]

CLOSE-UP

Is Your Body Language Revealing More Than You Want It To?

Don't look now—but someone may be reading your mind.

Actually, you should be looking, and paying attention to what you're seeing. Reading someone's nonverbal communication can give you important clues about what that person is thinking and feeling. Of course, the same applies to you. You might, for instance, be displaying a lack of confidence through nonverbal signals! Here are ten ways your body language may give the game away when you speak.

1. **Saying one thing and showing another.** Recently my family and I were having lunch at a restaurant in the neighboring state, and I asked the hostess for directions. She said, "Go out of the restaurant to the end of the block, then take a left," while indicating a *right* turn with her hand. I asked whether I should follow her words or her gesture. She laughed, realizing what she had done. The reason? It was probably just a momentary lack of attentiveness. If that happens in everyday situations, imagine how speaking in public can make you feel distracted. Stay focused!

2. **The "giveaway gesture."** Like micro-expressions (facial expressions that are often too fleeting to notice consciously), we can make gestures that betray our true feelings. When broadcast

journalist Diane Sawyer asked Amanda Knox in a televised interview if she'd been present during her roommate's murder in Italy, Ms. Knox answered "No," then immediately and emphatically nodded "*Yes*." Which of the conflicting signals would you believe? (Generally, people will trust a physical display over verbal content.)

3. **The vocal disconnect.** A recent article stated that financial analysts now pay close attention to the vocal patterns of public company CEOs on earnings calls. If an executive paints a rosy scenario for a stock's future performance, while at the same time *sounding* pessimistic, the analysts may not believe him or her. As with movement and gestures, listeners will trust vocal rather than verbal input. Enough *said*.

4. **"Leaving" listeners while you're thinking.** Have you noticed how some people look up at the ceiling or glance off to the side or at the floor while thinking about what they're going to say next? Whenever a speaker's gaze leaves an audience, listeners have a right to think, "Hey, I'm over here!" So, here's a general rule: *If you're not looking at your audience, nothing should be coming out of your mouth.*

5. **The deer-in-the-headlights look.** Among my clients are political candidates and officeholders. These politicians regularly face tough questions, and they need to look confident while responding. (The same, of course, goes for you and me.) Their facial expression—especially the look in their eyes—can reveal what's going on in their heads; and the last thing they need is an expression that says, "How do I respond to *that?*" So, I counsel them to think, "I can answer that!" The confidence shows in their eyes. Then I remind them to tie their response to the point they really want to make on this subject.

6. **Revealing that you're really not interested.** Do you pick up on cues that someone is totally uninterested in what you're saying? It's actually hard not to! By the same logic, you should avoid looking bored or condescending toward questions from your audience. Sometimes, we respond unkindly to people who just need a little more help in understanding us. Learn how to be

generous and kind to anyone who has shown you the respect to listen to you and then ask a question.

7. **Leaning away.** One of the worst pieces of body language advice (usually given by self-styled "experts") is that crossed arms indicate resistance. What if the person is shifting position to be more comfortable? What if the room is cold? Leaning away from someone may not necessarily mean avoidance, either. But if it's done for long enough or is abrupt, it can indicate a definite lack of engagement or agreement.

8. **Reluctance to communicate.** Occasionally in my work as a speech coach, I work with a client who has a tight jaw. This has to do with the spot where your lower jaw or *mandible* meets the upper jaw or *maxilla,* and consists of muscles and tendons that allow smooth movement. A tight jaw, on the other hand, can indicate a reluctance to communicate, since something appears to be keeping you from opening up. Are you in this tribe of tight-jawed speakers? If you are, massage the area until you can open your mouth more to let your wise words out!

9. **Excessive nodding.** Here's an interesting habit that you may not be aware of. If you nod while an audience member is asking a long question—especially if you begin doing it when the question *starts to become* long, or your nodding gets more vigorous—it's a subtle 'tell' that reveals this thinking: "Yes, okay. Would you please shut up now so I can answer the question?" Be careful of this body language!

10. **Staying away from your audience.** Physical obstacles like lecterns (podiums) make it hard to connect with audiences. Worse is when we ourselves create the metaphorical or actual distance. Pay attention to the configuration of your performance space. Then think about how to reduce the distance between you and listeners whenever possible. That may mean standing apart from a lectern, moving to a different part of the stage (hint: don't neglect the downstage area closest to the audience!), or even using the aisle(s). You do want to *reach* your listeners, don't you?

BODY LANGUAGE AND LEADERSHIP

Pride of Place in Speaking. Do you accept that when you speak, you're a leader? Regardless of the pecking order of those around you, you hold pride of place as the speaker. Thus, the stage is yours to command.

In fact, as an audience, we depend upon your ability to *lead us* through the ideas you're sharing with us. In Chapter 10, I discuss what I consider to be the essential qualities of speaking for leadership. For now, it's enough to know that you must display your leadership in taking us where you want us to go.

One of the ways you do this is through effective body language. It's a tool *par excellence* for controlling how others perceive you. If you accept the position of leadership as the speaker, you can't simply hope for the best in terms of how audience members think about you and your presentation.

Appropriate, strong body language leads directly to positive judgments about you and your message. Equally important, a robust physical presence helps make *our experience* of watching you a positive one. Of course, as speakers we can never be 100 percent certain of how audiences will respond to us. But why not enlist a tool that—in helping you command a stage—will bring you closer to how you want to be judged?

Another benefit: expansive body language in the presence of groups of people—that is, not being inhibited physically—increases your feelings of power and confidence and helps boost your self-image.[7] It's similar to the way you feel when you're "dressed for success," feeling confident with every step you take.

Here's a way to approximate that feeling onstage and to get yourself off to a solid start: *ground yourself.* That is, stand with both feet flat on the floor at about armpit-width. You'll immediately feel steadier and more stable than if you were standing casually or off-center—and you'll look steadfast. You will literally appear to be standing your ground. As audiences, we like that in a speaker.

How to Gesture for Public Speaking

Even though expansive body language can help you—especially in front of large audiences—your gestures should always be well defined and few in number. Think of it this way: for every additional gesture you use, what you say at the moment you use it is less memorable. In a stream of constant gesturing, which points will stand out?

Wherever possible, gestures should emanate from your center, i.e., they shouldn't involve arm or hand movements that are too far away from your body. Movements like that only dissipate energy and lessen visual impact. Gestures that come from "the center of who you are," on the other hand, are inherently powerful.

You also want your movements to look spontaneous and organic rather than planned. For that to happen, create the *conditions* for the gesture rather than the gesture itself. The thought you're having at this moment and the strength of your belief will make the movement look genuine. Then get in the habit of allowing your hands to fall back to your sides after the gesture. That's the "the neutral position," and it immediately makes your hands disappear from our consciousness.

When gestures are strong and infrequent, each one stands out and emphasizes the point you're making. That's the whole idea of gestures! Otherwise, you run the risk of your audience watching the three-ring circus that's going on with so much movement rather than paying attention to what you're saying.

How to Carry Yourself: What about the rest of the way you carry yourself? Remember, the impression you make starts before you begin speaking. If anyone in your group or audience knows that you are the speaker, the person will be watching and making decisions about you even before you open your mouth. In the world of the theater, this is often a painful lesson for young actors to learn, as they sometimes assume that audience members are only looking at the speaker and so they can slack off in terms of their own characterization. Audiences can and do look wherever they want at the scene in front of them not just at the person speaking!

Pay attention to your posture, and move smoothly. From those physical attributes, you'll be conveying both your comfort in the performance space and that you are in control. Be assured rather than timid in your movements—if you gesture, make it look like you mean it. Because body language is visual, it compels our attention at all times. But it also helps make what you say memorable because we equate what we're seeing with what we're hearing. If you've seen the movie *Titanic*, I'll bet you remember Kate Winslet spreading her arms wide as she stands on the prow of the massive racing vessel and shouting, "I'm flying!"

Two brilliant performers who were apparently able to convey total control by simply stepping on stage were operatic tenor Luciano Pavarotti and violinist Itzhak Perlman. One musical scholar was even compelled to ask what it was about their physical presence that so quickly mastered listeners. The answer, according to a survey he reports on, is "smooth, relaxed physical movements."[8]

What About Your Audience's Body Language?

Let me add one more point concerning your ability to use body language for leadership. In addition to a) grounding yourself, b) using strong and well-defined gestures, and c) carrying yourself with assuredness on stage, you need to pay attention to your audience's body language.

This often isn't a priority for speakers, who are mostly concerned with how they are doing (the speaker-centric syndrome). But of course, what matters is how the *audience* is doing, in terms of hearing and accepting what you say.

As psychologist and author Daniel Goleman reminds us, people mostly don't express their emotions verbally; they do so through other clues. His explanation: "The key to intuiting another's feelings is in the ability to read nonverbal channels: tone of voice, gesture, facial expression, and the like."[9] Naturally, when you're delivering a speech or presentation—except for the Q & A period—your audience won't be putting their thoughts and feelings into words. That's all the more reason you need to pay careful attention to their body language including facial expressions.

Confusion, resistance, skepticism, disagreement, and the like appearing in audience members' faces and bodies are signs that you need to take a different approach. Conversely, enthusiasm, rapt attentiveness, nodding, or smiling, are telling you that what you're saying at this moment resonates with your audience. If that's the case and you see listeners' clear interest, you may want to spend some time expanding upon that particular point with them.

THE BIOLOGICAL BASIS OF PERFORMANCE

As we've seen in these pages, biological factors have a role to play in both your performance and its reception by your audience. The brain-body connection is strong. Even as infants we learn that physical stimuli and responses (which we observe and imitate) are tied to intentions. And of course, the ability to read physical actions is an evolutionary trait that allows us to anticipate others' motives from their threatening or beneficial behaviors.

What should be obvious by this point is that there is a *biological basis* for the way ideas are transmitted from you as speaker to an audience. Your body language, in other words, is helping listeners not only to become more engaged, but also to understand your intentions concerning both your message and *them.*

In fact, it's even more fundamental than that. In the mid-1990s, scientists discovered something called the "mirror effect," which results from the presence of mirror neurons in the brain. These neurons are responsible for teaching us how to perform tasks by imitating what we see (like the infant, above, but this time throughout our lives). When we observe an action, mirror neurons in our brain fire as if we were performing the action ourselves. In other words, our brain responds as if our own body were completing the task!

It's the perfect example of how we embody intentions and emotions through physical actions. Equally important for us as speakers, *we help our audience experience our own emotions and intentions through our body language.*[10]

The Limbic System

The limbic brain—our emotional center—is "where the action is."[11] You may remember from Chapter 4 ("Overcoming Nerves and Speaking with Confidence") the limbic system's power to embed emotional memories.

The limbic system does this by responding to the environment around us, sending out signals to other parts of our brains. Because these signals concern survival and emotions, they are powerful, and naturally express themselves physically. If you walk into a park, for instance, the combination of being in a safe environment and the pleasure in the natural setting will embed this moment as an emotionally positive experience for you, and you may slow down and adapt more of a stroll than your typical purposeful walk. The limbic system, in fact, is the part of the brain that "plays the largest role in the expression of our nonverbal behavior."[12]

Let's bring that into speeches and presentations. If you are in touch with your emotions and attuned to the public speaking environment—in other words, if you are comfortable on stage—these signals and their physical expression will occur naturally and organically. But if you're uncomfortable or stressed out, that's the mindset you'll externalize on stage. And faked confidence usually isn't too hard to spot. Therefore, you shouldn't plan your gestures and movements to be a commanding presence; instead, allow them to arise organically. The more you are enjoying the moment in the spotlight, of course, the more that will show. Authenticity always announces itself loud and clear. It arises first in your own brain, then expresses itself in how you move and speak.

Speaking With Emotional Honesty. There's a direct connection here with acting. The reason audiences believe so readily in the characterization an actor is providing is because he or she is totally committed to living the life of that character. The actor *believes* in what is happening at the moment and lives it. She doesn't try to *show* us the character's response, which would be commenting on it. If we try to achieve the end result without taking the actual journey it will always look artificial and imposed, whether the performance is in acting or public speaking.

All of this is to say that natural expression—vocal, physical, and facial—arises from true belief and commitment, or what we might call *emotional honesty*. If you believe and accept emotionally what you're saying, all of the ways you try to get it across will be honest and true. Your limbic system is always closely connected to how you view and respond to the world. If you can pair that connection with *what you show*, you will be dynamic and believable while speaking on stage.

Expressing Yourself, Moment by Moment

So, how can you accomplish this in practical performance terms as a speaker? You can do so by allowing yourself to experience what's happening *moment by moment* as you speak. Tune into all of the stimuli that are coming your way—your own sense of your body in space, your breathing, and the sound of your voice. Respond to the physical environment you share with the audience. Watch your listeners' reactions. If you're speaking virtually and there isn't a shared space or you can't see the listeners, pay particular attention to how the ideas of your presentation are changing, and use those changes as new stimuli (as in fact they are!). Feel the pace of your presentation, and control it. There's a dance going on between you and your audience. Participate, and enjoy it!

Too often we're so absorbed in our desire to do well that we don't pay attention to each moment that we and the audience are experiencing together. Sometimes, in our nervousness at an upcoming talk, we over-prepare with a too-carefully constructed presentation *so that nothing can go wrong*. Then we roll it out *in spite* of the audience, so that we're not responding to the speaking moment at all!

If you open yourself up to it instead—if you let the moment happen—you'll connect with your limbic system, which is all about processing the moment and shaping your emotional response to it. Don't worry about losing control over your material. If you know your stuff, you'll be able to deliver the content to listeners more naturally than a rigid presentation ever could.

Your limbic brain is an incredible tool that helps give you presence, provided that you listen to what it's telling you. The result can be physical expressiveness that is perfectly calibrated for the moment at hand.

EXTERNALIZING WHAT YOU FEEL

One of the most valuable lessons you as a business speaker can learn from the art of theatrical performance is this need to physically express what you're thinking and feeling. You must show outwardly what's going on inside you so that your audience can think and feel the same things themselves. Remember the power of mirror neurons to make this happen.

This ability to externalize what's inside you is perhaps the central skill of acting, and it's a quality that is often lacking in public speakers. It's not hard to understand why this is so. Actors train and rehearse their entire professional lives to be able to physically externalize mental and emotional states. It's a skill of spoken performance that, sadly, almost no one in business is ever exposed to.

Accept this truth then: if you want to achieve leadership presence, you must speak in the language of the body as well as that of the mind. Body language is the art of physical expression, and it's as vital to your influence as anything you say.

How to Be at Ease Using Body Language. Want an easy way to adopt this powerful tool while increasing your comfort level in front of an audience? Imagine you're welcoming listeners into your home. You know what it's like to be at ease in your own environment, welcoming friends through the front door. Use this visualization to bring your audience into the space (real or vitual) that you'll be occupying together.

If you can project that level of comfort, audiences will feel they're in good hands. And why not? What they'll see and hear is your true voice and natural physical expression on a topic everyone is interested in. In the best way possible, you'll be 'embodying' the content you're sharing with them.

BUILDING TRUST AND EMPATHY: FACIAL EXPRESSIONS

To conclude this chapter on body language and physical display, I'd like to talk about facial expressions. This is often a neglected topic when it comes to understanding the body in performance.

If you're like most people, you focus mainly on your gestures when it comes to using body language for public speaking. But what your face is showing gives your audience important clues about everything from your passion for the topic to whether you're a trustworthy messenger. And believe me, audiences are keenly aware of what they're seeing and how it relates to their own needs. Animals rely on a keen sense of smell for recognition and to sense danger. But we *watch* each other's faces and bodies to try to understand feelings and intentions.

And the face is easily as expressive as the body! We're capable of thousands of facial expressions, including fifty different types of smiles.[13] Therefore, as a speaker, you need a sense of what your own face is showing in performance.

Is your face flexible enough to show what you're feeling? Or do you lack much facial expression? Public speaking isn't a poker game where the object is to hide what you're thinking! And when you do show emotion, are your expressions appropriate?

A key question for any speaker is whether audiences are seeing what he or she is really thinking. No speaker wants listeners to have a false impression based on what his or her face is showing. Many of my clients, in fact, are shocked when they see themselves on video. They are often observing for the first time not only what they look like overall, but what they're sending out as facial signals. If it's the opposite of what they intended, it can be quite unsettling.

To see this in action, try videotaping or screen-recording yourself on a topic you typically speak on. Make sure the topic is important to you—the more heartfelt advocacy it involves, the better. Deliver your remarks as though you were actually speaking in a real-life situation. Just before you watch yourself, turn off the volume or mute the microphone on your screen. Now you'll be paying more attention to your face than your content. (Also, for this exercise, try to focus on your face rather than your gestures.)

Imagine you're an audience member watching this speaker, i.e., you. Ask yourself the following questions. (1) What are you seeing in terms of this person's commitment to their message? (2) How strongly do you think she or he wants to get it across? (3) Do they seem to genuinely care about this topic? (4) Am I seeing anything that reveals how this speaker feels about his or her listeners?

You can also enlist the help of friends and colleagues by asking them what you seem to be showing facially. It can be startling at times to hear that you're showing an emotion you're not feeling at all. ("Why did you seem angry?")

Essential Speaking Tools

It could be that you've learned to control your facial expressions. (Remember your mother saying, *"Don't you show that face to me!"*) If that's the case and you lack much facial expression, that's an area you should work on. Otherwise, you'll be missing a prime opportunity for an emotional connection with your audience. Practicing with a mirror or video recording can help you match what you feel and what you're showing. At some point, muscle memory will allow you to feel the expression that your face assumes when you're experiencing a particular emotion.

One problem is that we often "leak" our true emotions through fleeting facial giveaways, because we are responding to our emotional brain's rapid response tool. These revealing displays are called *micro expressions*, a term coined by psychologist and nonverbal communication expert Paul Ekman.

The important point here is, that you don't want to literally wear a false face for your audience. The face is part of your essential speaking toolkit because it can convey subtle nuances of emotion. It is indeed a canvas on which we show what we're thinking and feeling, making us "the most expressive animals on this planet."[14] When your facial expressions match the content of what you're talking about, your speech becomes infinitely easier to understand in all of its dimensions.

Don't be afraid to show it to us facially as well as in your body.

STILLNESS AND POWER

I have one last thought to conclude this chapter on physical expressiveness. Powerful stage presence starts with *stillness*. Stillness conveys confidence and control. The speaker who begins with stillness moves precisely when she or he feels the need to do so.

Just as people who babble incessantly come across as insecure next to the person who is still and composed, the nervous performer merely calls attention to the uncontrolled nature of superfluous movement.

The art of physical expression comes from being in touch with what you say, how you feel about it, and how you express it bodily. After that, it's just a case of being open enough to pour it all out to those listening so they get it. Keep these thoughts in mind and your physical performance will be dynamic and effective.

CLOSE-UP

The Body Language Rules:™
12 Ways to Be a More Powerful Speaker

Successful speaking is about power used benevolently. Good speakers don't manipulate audiences. But they realize that they must exert control at every turn: over the material; the pacing and timing; the audience's response; and their own body.

Here are my "Body Language Rules." They are twelve powerful ways you can use nonverbal communication to make yourself a more credible and dynamic speaker.

1. **If You Have a Choice, Stand.** Your body is such a vital communication tool that it's a shame to deprive your audience of 50 percent of it. Yet that's what happens when you sit down to make a presentation. Full-body movements are part of your power.

2. **Ground Yourself.** "Grounding," means to assume a strong stance, with your feet at armpit-width and your weight evenly distributed. Setting yourself like this gives you the appearance of stability. *You and your ideas* will appear steadfast.

3. **Keep Your Arms in "Neutral".** Self-consciousness on stage can turn you into a statue or at the other extreme, an octopus. Start with your arms at your sides—that's the "neutral position." Bring the arms up to make a strong gesture then let them disappear again by bringing them back down to your sides.

4. **Use Open Body Positions.** Crossing your arms or locking your hands creates a physical barrier between you and your listeners. Instead, keep your body language open so there's literally nothing between you and the audience. Influence and rapport can then flow unimpeded from you straight to your listeners.

5. **When Seated, Sit Straight and Slightly Forward.** Let's say you have to sit. Bring your butt one-third of the way forward on the seat, and lean in slightly. You'll look professional and interested. Leaning back will make you look comfy and unengaged.

6. **Make Your Gestures Spare and Clean.** Don't worry about using your hands too much. But gesture *only* when you feel the need to emphasize something. Each gesture will be strong and "clean" in the sense of being well defined. It will possess its own power.

7. **Move with Purpose.** Some speakers wander like a cloud; others pace like a tiger. You, instead, should move with purpose. For instance, move just *before* you start a new talking point. Or use the slide screen as a destination to point something out. Visuals like this help boost an audience's interest and retention.

8. **Love Your Audience More than You Do Your Notes.** You're not here to read to people. It's time to share what you know

and who you are. The exact words you say don't matter—it's your intent to get it across that's important. If you want to influence people, look at them. Easy to remember, and something that will make your presentation easier for you in the end.

9. **Love Your Audience More than You Do Your Slide Show.** The screen won't love you back! Pay more attention to those you're persuading than you do to reading data or bullet points. If you have to remind yourself of what comes next in your narrative by looking at a slide, you're not ready to take this show on the road.

10. **The Podium (Lectern) Is in Your Way.** The lectern is a roadblock impeding the delivery of your message. Don't hang on it, lean on it, or rest your hands on it—you need them to gesture. The solution? Step away from the lectern whenever you can, so you're fully visible and free to *move*.

11. **'Welcome' Questioners.** If you're lucky enough to have people question you or pose challenges to what you're saying, you should make them feel welcome. Avoid pointing a finger at a questioner while saying: *"Yes?"* Use an open palm gesture instead.

12. **"Are You Gonna Shoot That Gun or Just Wave It Around, Cowpoke?"** Ever watch a presenter who holds a flip chart or whiteboard marker but never uses it? A variation is the speaker who gets up to speak and forgets that he is still clutching his pen. Don't keep audiences waiting in vain for you to use the writing instrument you're wielding! They'll be paying that much less attention to what you're saying.

Nonverbal communication can be as important as your verbal content. Learn to use it to your advantage. After all, a body is a terrible thing to waste.

CHAPTER 8

Grab 'Em in Sixty Seconds! — How to Start a Speech

I see you stand like greyhounds in the slips,
Straining upon the start. The game's afoot.

—Shakespeare, Henry V

You never get a second chance to make a first impression.

—Will Rogers

By this point in *Speak for Leadership*, you should have a thorough understanding of my system that underlies speaking with power and presence. Let's review what's been covered so far:

Chapter 1 examined how anyone can learn stage presence and that it's not a gift you're either granted at birth or not. The next chapter, Chapter 2, showed how you're a natural performer and can easily transform those skills into more dynamic speaking. Chapter 3 discussed ways in which you can make yourself memorable and Chapter 4 showed you how to overcome nerves and speak with confidence. As we've seen, demonstrating confidence alone can make you a more credible and believable speaker.

In Chapter 5, I discussed the central importance of breathing for more focused and powerful public speaking. The following chapters looked at two of your greatest performance assets: your voice (Chapter 6), and body language and physical expression (Chapter 7).

These chapters covered the philosophy of gaining stage presence to speak for leadership and the assets at your command for doing so. They examined thoughts and attitudes, including your relationship with your audience; and the brain and emotional input—again, both yours and your listeners'. And they showed how you must draw upon your physical resources—voice, face, and body—to be an exciting and memorable presence on stage. You may have understood some of this material before you started reading this book. But I'd guess that much of it was a surprise to you in terms of developing leadership presence for public speaking.

I'm going to shift gears now. My focus going forward will be on the *practical speech elements* that will help make you a successful speaker. First, I'll discuss how to start a speech for maximum impact. Storytelling used to tap into your audience's emotional response will be a core element of that discussion. I'll also talk about your introduction's twin – your conclusion – in achieving influence. Next, I'll share with you the seven essential qualities of speaking for leadership. I'll then follow up with the most powerful ways to command a stage. In the final chapter, I'll develop a concept that I think is an ideal finish to a book about relating to and influencing listeners: how to make any audience love you.

How *do* you deal with what is likely to be the most important moment in your performance—whether it's a presentation, sales pitch, lecture, interview, meeting, or off-the-cuff remarks? How do you start a speech in a way that hooks your audience and makes them eager, even excited, to hear what you have to say?

THE POWER OF FIRST IMPRESSIONS

How long does it take for someone to form an impression of you, anyway? I think most of us these days would say it probably takes only seconds. The immense portion of our lives we spend in the digital world has speeded up our responses that much. And though it's always been the case that we make snap-judgments about people, today it seems to be happening faster than ever. As you can understand, that type of response plays out in how listeners react to you when you speak.

Why You Need to Hit the Ground Running

How many times have you said to friends or colleagues, "Well, I was nervous for the first couple of minutes. But after that, I hit my groove and everything was fine." But audiences are making decisions about you at lightning speed. That means you have to hit the ground running— even though this is the moment when you're apt to be most nervous and self-conscious. I call this time of feeling like a sitting duck, "the awful first two minutes."

The truth is that audiences are responding to physical and social cues without even being aware that such a process is taking place. The part of the brain that's responsible? It's our old friend from my discussion on overcoming fear of public speaking: the amygdala. Since the amygdala is all about emotional response, it's not only the center of fear for all of us. It's also where we make emotionally based decisions about people.

A friend of mine, Nancy Boudreaux, shared some fascinating information in this regard. Nancy works for the State of Louisiana preventing financial fraud following natural disasters—like Hurricane Katrina. She says studies have shown that when some elderly investors have age-related changes in the amygdala, they can't discern "untrustworthy" faces. They're likely to fall victim to financial scams not because they're more gullible than younger subjects (who don't have this problem), but because their brains don't pick up on visual cues.

As we know by now, speaking with presence includes tapping into an audience's emotional response (a reaction that the people mentioned in the previous paragraph had difficulty with). It's easy, then, to grasp why so many speeches and presentations fail: the speakers concern themselves only with delivering information. While those speakers get the data right, they ignore a vital part of their influence: allowing the audience to respond emotionally to what they're hearing.

HOW TO START A SPEECH

Once you know the above, the conclusion becomes inescapable. You must achieve emotional and intellectual engagement of listeners *at the start* to launch your speech successfully, no later than the first thirty to sixty seconds. In other words, you need to aim for immediate and maximum impact. If strong engagement and a willingness to listen by the audience don't take place at your opening, when will they? The answer is probably at no time. Right from the start you need to—as I call it—"open the door to influence."

Let's discuss how to open your speeches in ways that:

1. Engage your audience immediately;

2. Open a channel of communication;

3. Arouse everyone's interest enough to truly listen;

4. Alert them that your topic relates to their lives; and

5. Show them you're going to be interesting.

That's a hefty list of positive results to achieve in the first minute!

THE 5 KEY INGREDIENTS OF SUCCESSFUL PRESENTATIONS

Think of the five elements that follow as "key ingredients" to successful presentations, whoever your audience is. These ingredients will put you on the path I described above. They work for all types of speaking: speeches, informal talks, lectures, keynotes, pitches, and more—and they're easy to implement. Best of all, they support the two reasons you're speaking to an audience in the first place: (1) to deliver an important message in an interesting way, and (2) to prepare listeners to take the action you're aiming for.

Key Ingredient #1: Your Greeting

Imagine you work in the Accounts Receivable department of a hospital. A potential vendor delivers the following sales pitch to your team:

> "Good morning. I'm Glenn Collect-More, president of Collect-More Medical Billing. Our experts help hospitals and medical groups maximize practice revenue. I'm delighted to speak to you this morning. Would you like to increase the number of paying patients you process while reducing your workload?"

Looks okay written out like that, doesn't it? But now imagine that this salesman took a grand total of *fourteen seconds* to say all of that. That's exactly what took place at a presentation skills workshop I conducted recently at a hospital association conference. (The speaker's name above is fictitious, of course.) Remember, this was the first thing that the volunteer in my workshop—an actual salesman for a medical billing company—said to his audience of hospital Accounts Receivable personnel. In other words, it was his *greeting*.

What was wrong with it?

Well, I should tell you that aside from the fact that he raced through what he was saying, his voice was flat and uninflected—what I call a "vocal plateau." There was no expressiveness, inflection, or coloration in his voice to allow his words to "light up" in listeners' minds. (For the best techniques for vocal expressiveness, review the Close-up in Chapter 6: "The 5 Key Tools of Vocal Dynamics.") This was true even though the speaker and everyone in the audience had a professional interest in his topic!

So how successful would you say his greeting was?

Your Greeting: The Often-Forgotten Presentation Element

Your *greeting* is important because it's the first ingredient of an effective opening. You may have heard in high school that a speech has three parts: introduction, body, and conclusion. But actually, there's almost always a fourth element—the greeting.

The greeting matters because it introduces both you and your topic to your audience. It gives listeners a flavor of what will follow. Equally important, it opens up the channel of communication between you and them, alerting your audience that what you are saying (and are about to say) matters to them. And it primes listeners to pay maximum attention to you because it shows that you're prepared, professional, and purpose-driven.

Your greeting, in other words, is all about *a relationship*. It's the only time you'll be speaking to these people directly and not through the filter of your content. So, it's vital that you connect with them rather than just jumping into agendas, slides, and data.

Don't neglect your greeting as many speakers do! And please, when you say you're delighted to be there, make it sound genuine and not like something you're supposed to say. You'd be amazed at how many speakers fall into this trap.

Make Sure You Play Every Note

Here's another consideration regarding your greeting: it's not all one utterance. It consists of discrete parts, each of which tells your audience something. And since audiences make judgments about you very quickly—in the first thirty to sixty seconds—it's vital that you get this right.

For instance, let's take a closer look at Mr. 'Collect-More's' opening.

By now (we can assume) that as a salesman, he's delivered this pitch so many times that he may have a tendency to fly through it—which is exactly what he did. Information rattled off like that can hardly have much meaning for an audience!

So, in this workshop, I pointed out to my volunteer Mr. 'Collect-More' and the attendees, that there were actually *five* components to his greeting—and each one required its own focus. Consider, for instance, that before he got to the important question that he had formulated to hook his audience ("Would you like to increase the number of paying patients you process while reducing your workload?"), he had done all of the following:

1. Acknowledged everyone by saying "Good morning."

2. Gave his name and title.

3. Identified his company's expertise.

4. Expressed his pleasure at being there.

Only after he had accomplished these four things, did he get to the fifth component: his all-important question, meant to get listeners to identify with everything else he was about to say.

Do You 'Invest Yourself' in What You're Saying? I coached this volunteer for five minutes or so in front of everyone. What I was trying to do was to get him to *invest himself* emotionally in each element of his greeting.

And in just that brief amount of coaching time, he began to match his content with his vocal delivery. Doing so accomplished two important tasks: a) allowed each element to live on its own in terms of what it was trying to achieve, and b) slowed the speaker down enough to make his content sound more genuine. In fact, the workshop audience spontaneously applauded his last attempt! He had progressed to delivering a greeting that accomplished its job: launching his presentation strongly.

Remember: your greeting allows you to connect with your audience. Take your time with it, and let your enthusiasm show. Your speech or presentation actually starts here, not at the moment you discuss your first main point.

Key Ingredient #2: The Grabber

Imagine this scenario: You've finally been invited to pitch to the management of a big-ticket prospect. It's a moment you've been working toward for the past year. There's no doubt that it's a high-stakes, high-reward appearance for you as sales director. In response, you've put together a killer presentation that should knock everyone's socks off.

There's just one problem: you have no idea how to start off with a bang. You know your opening must compel everybody's attention. You're just not sure *how*.

When it comes to influencing listeners in speeches and presentations, two concepts explain why the beginning and ending need to be particularly strong. I'll discuss both concepts briefly then provide some powerful tools for your opening gambit: your speech's introduction. Later in this chapter, I'll discuss the bookend: your conclusion.

We saw in the last section that the greeting sets the tone of your presentation. It should also accomplish some other necessary tasks, including providing necessary information, displaying your professionalism, and demonstrating your enthusiasm. Now let's talk about what needs to take place in the presentation itself.

Primacy and Recency: The two essential concepts governing your opening and closing are *primacy* and *recency*. "Primacy" states that people remember most vividly what they experience at the beginning of a speech. "Recency" says that those same people will strongly recall what you give them at the end. In terms of public speaking, these essential moments translate into your introduction and conclusion.

THE INTRODUCTION

Here are three reasons why your introduction needs to be engaging and interesting *immediately*:

1. Audiences make value judgments about you, your organization, and your message within the first minute at most. (Note that this time interval includes your greeting.) After this point, you'll be able to change people's opinions about as easily as you can change a hamster into a ham sandwich.

2. Your opening sets the entire tone of your presentation—including whether you're likely to be interesting or not.

3. The first minute is when you introduce your message and tell the audience why they need to listen *because it will benefit them, make their lives easier, etc.* In this short space of time, listeners need to be both engaged and predisposed favorably toward you and your message. Neither outcome will occur unless you can grab their attention sufficiently so they're poised to listen to your verbal magic.

You Can Be Creative, Can't You?

To engage an audience instantly, your speaking toolkit needs to be stocked with some careful thinking and a bit of imagination. The good news is that, since you know your topic well and you're already primed for creating influence, you're well positioned to succeed.

Primacy won't have much of a chance to operate, on the other hand, if you use the dreary "Today, I'd like to talk about…" opening. This is a dreadfully boring way to begin, and you should remove it from your public speaking toolbox permanently.

Since you know your topic well, a few minutes of focused thinking should be all you need to plan how to launch your topic intelligently and engagingly. Do that, and your talk won't sound like every other one that's ever been given in your industry.

As a springboard to verve and originality, here are a dozen reliable devices that work well as speech hooks or *grabbers*.

12 Great Grabbers (To Hook Any Audience)

- Question
- Story
- Quotation
- Visual
- Statistic
- Startling statement
- Personal anecdote or experience

- Humor
- Expert opinion
- Today's newspaper headline or major social media hashtag
- Physical object or demonstration
- Client testimonial or other success story

You could think of many more openings from your own expertise or the world of your audience. The best grabbers engage listeners right away in terms of intellect AND emotions. The easiest way to come up with one is to consider who your listeners are and what turns them on.

It's true that coming up with an effective grabber involves some work. But the rewards if you're successful more than justify the effort.

Want some examples? Here are some powerful grabbers—each one illustrating a category listed above:

Jesus, Sermon on the Mount: "Blessed are the poor in spirit: for theirs is the kingdom of heaven." (Startling statement.)

Bill Clinton, 1993 speech in Memphis to ministers (after having heard himself introduced as "Bishop Clinton"): "You know, in the last ten months, I've been called a lot of things, but nobody's called me a bishop yet. When I was about nine years old, my beloved and now departed grandmother, who was a very wise woman, looked at me and she said, 'You know, I believe you could be a preacher if you were just a little better boy.'" (Humor)

Jane Fonda, TED Talk on "Life's Third Act": "There have been many revolutions over the last century, but perhaps none as significant as the longevity revolution. We are living on average today thirty-four years longer than our great-grandparents did. Think about that: that's an entire second adult lifetime that's been added to our lifespan." (Statistic.)

Patrick Buchanan, 1995 speech announcing his presidential campaign: "Three years ago when I came to New Hampshire, I went up to the North Country on one of my first visits. I went up to the James River paper mill. It was a bad day, just before Christmas, and many of the workers at the plant had just been laid off. They were sullen and they were angry and they didn't want to talk to anyone. So, as I walked down that line of workers, I will never forget: Men shook my hand and looked away. Then, one of them, with his head down, finally looked up, and with tears in his eyes said, 'Save our jobs.' When I got back to Manchester that night, I read a story in the *Union Leader* about the United States Export-Import Bank funding a new paper mill in Mexico. What are we doing to our own people?" (Story + rhetorical question...with a powerful emotional pull.)

Key Ingredient #3: Eye Contact

As we've seen, audiences make decisions about your credibility, believability, and likability within the first thirty to sixty seconds. Actually, if you're visible before you speak—if you're sitting on stage waiting to be introduced, for instance, or if you greet audience members beforehand—these decisions start even earlier.

It's your *physical presence* that audience members are responding to. And we all know that impressions based on body language can be powerful. To be sure you're broadcasting the right nonverbal communication when you speak, you need to display effective body language from the start. That means relating to the presence of your audience. And that in turn involves using strong eye contact and acknowledging the listeners' presence in physical terms.

Why Eye Contact Matters

For most of us, the first few minutes facing an audience is a stressful time. And we seek comfort wherever we can find it—including our notes or slide deck. Basically, we'll do anything to avoid looking back at that group of strangers staring at us!

But as we've seen, the moments when you greet your audience and launch your presentation are vital to establishing a relationship with them. Once again, then, the important rule I mentioned earlier, stated slightly differently this time:

> *If you're looking down at your notes,*
> *nothing should be coming out of your mouth.*

In speeches where you must read from a manuscript, teach yourself how to look down and "capture" phrases and sentences that embody the key idea. Then look up at your listeners and say it. It's the ideas you express that will be exciting to them, not how you perfectly read a perfect manuscript. *You need to be looking at people when you share important ideas with them.* You can't bury your nose in some written material when you have people to persuade and motivate.

Remember those critical first sixty seconds!

Interestingly, relating to an audience this way allows each person to think you're talking to them individually. They can then respond attentively to your conversation with them. Just because people are gathered in a group doesn't mean they lose their individuality.

One other thing concerning eye contact: Look at each audience member long enough so that real contact is made. A couple of seconds is long enough for this to occur. Avoid "flicking" your gaze at people in less-than-a-second intervals just because you've heard that you need to look at everyone at some point.

If you're addressing a really large audience, aim your gaze to geographic sections. Make sure you include the entire house (though not in a noticeable pattern). Because each person is far away from you, it will seem like you're looking directly at them when you turn toward the section in which they're sitting.

Key Ingredient #4: Humor

In virtually every speaking situation, humor or a light touch will help you achieve your purpose. That's true even if you employ the tactic only occasionally, or in the context of an otherwise serious speech.

There's no doubt that humor can be an entertaining and persuasive public speaking tool. However, unless people start laughing the moment you enter a room, you shouldn't give humor the central role in your talk. That advice holds up even for after-dinner speeches, which are supposed to be entertaining. Any humor in your speeches still has to serve your goal, just like every other element of your talk. In other words: it's better to say something worthwhile without humor, than to be funny while not sharing anything profound.

How Humor Can Help You as a Speaker

Let's look at how humor can aid your speaking success. I'll also touch upon the places where the ice gets a little thin.

Jeff Fleming said this about humor in the pages of *Professional Speaker,* the journal of the National Speakers Association: "Humor makes an audience more receptive to your message, improves retention of points made, reduces tension, improves creativity and provides entertainment value to any presentation."[1]

Sounds like a pretty good speaking tool, doesn't it? I'll add this: humor allows your audience to see you as human and to identify with you. And it lets everybody in the room have some fun at the same time. But how in the world can you incorporate humor? If you step back and take a look at a) your topic, b) the speaking situation, c) the audience, or d) the work you do or your personal life, you should easily be able to find something humorous to include in your speech. Believe me, there's something quirky, ridiculous, absurd, embarrassing, or entertaining in at least one of those four.

Like any presentation element, however, humor should be used in moderate doses. And it absolutely has to fit in with your message! Here's a real-life example of what happens when neither situation is in place:

ARE YOU JOKING? A few years ago, I conducted a corporate workshop at a large medical manufacturer. The trainees were the vice presidents of a dozen different departments: finance, sales, quality control, distribution, etc. On the workshop's second day, each exec was required to give a ten-minute presentation. We videotaped the talks then I opened up the floor after each one for instructor- and peer critiques. One of the VPs opted to open with a joke. This turned out to be a stretch-limo of a joke that took up *three and a half minutes* of his allotted ten-minute time. And this joke's central character was . . . the *Pope!*

How's that for living dangerously?

Four Valuable Lessons (That Ain't Funny!) This true story contains four valuable lessons concerning telling a joke instead of incorporating humor: (1) Your effort shouldn't take up so much time that it competes with the body of your presentation. (2) It should be culturally appropriate. (3) What you say must be related to your topic. And (4) Well thought-out humor is generally safe, while a joke spells T-R-O-U-B-L-E.

Why are jokes trouble? Well, telling a joke takes good timing. Also, you probably need the ability to create some voice characterizations. Most important: a joke is a zero-sum game. It either succeeds or falls flat, which is embarrassing for everyone present. Jokes are really worlds away from the shared perceptions and interests you're trying to establish with this audience.

So, use humor, and keep it relevant, gentle, and in good taste.

Key Ingredient #5: The Clincher

Remember the concepts of primary and recency that I mentioned above? Again, *primacy* states that audiences will retain best what they experience first; and *recency* says that your listeners will strongly remember what you say last. These two concepts have great importance when it comes to creating impactful public speaking.

I mentioned earlier that a speaker who starts out with the all-too-common, "Today I'd like to talk about…" or "I've been asked to speak on the topic of…" is really just droning on before he or she even gets started. It's an early sign that such a presenter is probably not going to deliver a talk that sings.

The smart speaker, on the other hand, will intrigue and perhaps surprise listeners. That in fact is the purpose of the grabbers I listed above. The same principle—say something unexpected, unusual, and/or thought provoking so that your ideas resonate in everyone's mind—also applies to the way in which you *end* your speech.

A Word or Two Before You Go

Since recency states that listeners will likely retain the last thing you say, you want to make your ending sticky. "Quit while you're ahead," and "Always leave 'em laughing," are two well-known sayings that embody the idea that a speech should end on a powerful note.

Now, think about the conclusions to all the speeches and presentations you've listened to over the past year. How many of them were memorable? How many of them even *had* a conclusion?

One of the most common public speaking errors, in fact, is the lack of a memorable closing that drives home the speaker's message. The body of your speech is the entrée, and it should be delicious and nourishing. But do you really want to leave your audience without any dessert?

Just as you grabbed the audience's attention at the start of your speech, you need a memorable conclusion that refocuses everyone on your message. As with your introduction, a solid conclusion requires some thought and a dash of creativity on your part. But here's good news: The same list of springboard openings I mentioned on pages 136–138 as grabbers can also be used to conclude your speech! The principle is the same: you need to say or show something dramatic or provocative that stays in the audience's mind afterwards. If your conclusion includes a call to action, so much the better.

Here's some more help: In addition to those dozen devices I've already mentioned, here is a "Triple-T" combination of rhetorical devices which can be part of a powerful clincher. Consider using one of them:

- Thesis-Antithesis
- Triad (any group of three)
- Tribute

Here they are in action in some famous examples:

- John F. Kennedy, Inaugural Address (1961): "And so, my fellow Americans: ask not what your country can do for you—ask what you can do for your country. My fellow citizens of the world: ask not what America will do for you, but what together we can do for the freedom of man." (Thesis-Antithesis)
- Abraham Lincoln, Gettysburg Address (1863): "It is rather for us to be here dedicated to the great task remaining before us— that from these honored dead we take increased devotion to that cause for which they gave the last full measure of devotion— that we here highly resolve that these dead shall not have died in vain—that this nation, under God, shall have a new birth of freedom—and that government of the people, by the people, for the people, shall not perish from the earth. (Triad)

- First Lady Ladybird Johnson's 1964 speech on Eleanor Roosevelt: "Let us today earnestly resolve to build the true foundation for **Eleanor Roosevelt's** memory—to pluck out prejudice from our lives, to remove fear and hate where it exists, and to create a world unafraid to work out its destiny in peace. **Eleanor Roosevelt** has already made her own splendid and incomparable contribution to that foundation. Let us go and do likewise, within the measure of our faith and the limits of our ability. Let **Eleanor Roosevelt** teach us all how to turn the arts of compassion into the victories of democracy. (Tribute)

And you noticed as well the two *triads* in that last example, didn't you? (I only bolded one of them so you could find the other!)

CLOSE-UP

How to Make Your Case in 30 Seconds or Less

Would you like to meet the world's greatest influencer? Ladies and gentlemen, allow me to introduce...*television*.

Even though early TV comic Ernie Kovacs joked, "Television is a medium because it is neither rare nor well done," the small screen has always been quite a dazzler. In addition, it can persuade us fast and reliably. Among the other things that TV has taught us, is that visuals are powerful tools for persuasion.

So, if you're a speaker who wants to influence quickly—say, within the thirty to sixty seconds it takes for an audience to start judging you—you can learn from television's techniques. It will help you to *broadcast* a message that is concise and impactful and that includes a visual component. Just follow the five steps below.

1. **Decide on your objective.** To be clear on what you're trying to achieve, take a look at the persuasive tool par excellence of television: the commercial. Commercials *show* us a solution to our need in visual terms, and with extreme conciseness. Sponsors can do this efficiently because they are ultra-clear on their objective: to get us to buy what they're selling *because we've seen*

our problem solved right in front of us. Suffering from heartburn because of that chili you had for dinner? Here's the antacid you need—and look at it going to work! (Cue in animation of a fire in someone's belly, instantly extinguished by the antacid solution they just swallowed.)

Ask yourself, therefore, before you think about the content you're going to include in your presentation: *"What do I want my listeners to think, feel, or do as a result of my speech?"* Your job is never to inform or explain. It's always to move audiences to your side of the street!

2. **Use an effective hook.** Think of a commercial you enjoy watching (come on, you know you have at least one). The first time you saw it, weren't you intrigued right away at the beginning of the spot? Didn't the quirky, startling, visually funny, or outrageous nature of the ad pull you right in?

    In terms of your own talks, remember that your central message won't resonate unless people are still with you when you get to it. If you hook their interest at the start, there's a reasonable chance that they'll still be there mentally at the right moment. If you don't, they probably won't.

3. **State the problem and its solution clearly.** Here's a classic TV commercial you've seen from different brands. It's a series of images: (1) A four-year-old boy, chasing the family's new puppy in the backyard and falling all over the place. (Or stomping around in a puddle with his rain boots and covering himself with mud; or laughing and tumbling on the front lawn and acquiring lots of grass stains, etc., etc.) (2) Mom holding up his stained clothes with a pained expression…or an ironic smile. (3) Shot of box of washing machine detergent, or Mom pouring liquid from a measuring cup into the washer. (4) Mom smiling as she holds up the same pair of pants, now sparkling clean.

    We get it all: a problem and its solution presented as succinctly as possible, without any wasted time or dialogue. Television does this kind of thing seamlessly with visuals. As a speaker, you need to use visuals too. And I'm referring here not only to the things you show listeners. You must also *speak visually,* as in the next step.

4. **Paint word pictures.** Studies have shown that visual stimuli can be the most dynamic element of persuasive communication. That means you must not only use visuals when you present your ideas; you must also speak in visuals.

   What does this mean? If you paint a picture with language the scene may captivate listeners in a way that plain data-based words alone can't match. For instance, there's a vast difference between: "We need to make our product the favorite toy this holiday season," and *"Imagine children all over the country, opening their kept-until-last present on Christmas morning. They tear off the giftwrap…and their eyes open wide. They realize they now have the ONE THING they were hoping Santa would bring them—OUR TOY!"*

5. **Tell a story.** When time is short and you need to make a point quickly, nothing is as powerful as a story. (The Christmas morning event described above is a mini-story.) A story immediately engages and convinces in ways that dry information or numbers can't. Tell a story and you're saying, "Look, I don't want to just throw some data at you. Let me show you what this means in terms of human beings and their conflicts and triumphs."

   The story you tell, with human motives and eventual success will make the same information come to life. Again, think of those mini-stories in commercials, TV dramas, or sitcoms that show how people are affected.

   So, open up your book of stories. You won't have any problem finding good ones if you just pay attention to what's happening with the people in your company, industry, or community. Share those stories and you'll have listeners hooked—all within that critical first sixty seconds.

CHAPTER 9

Storytelling to Create an Emotional Response

Out of the fullness of the heart, the mouth speaks.

—Matthew 12:34

The truthful, inside story of almost any man's life—if told modestly and without offending egotism—is most entertaining. It is almost sure-fire speech material.

—Dale Carnegie

Can I tell you a story? It's all about how you can captivate audiences so they're engaged, attuned to you emotionally, and eager to hear what you have to say.

Doesn't that sound like an essential part of speaking presence?

Chances are you already know that storytelling is a vital element of memorable public speaking. But, do you know how this approach works as well as how to use it effectively?

Why Stories Matter

We looked briefly at telling a story at the end of the last chapter, in terms of making your case in sixty seconds or less. But stories aren't only helpful when you're under the speechwriting gun. Storytelling is one of the best tools you have for making people realize that what you're saying matters to their lives.

Simply put, speakers with leadership presence tell stories.

It's all part of effective performance. And telling stories is so ingrained in the human experience, that it certainly isn't limited to public speaking. Think of a parent (perhaps yourself) telling a child a story to teach him or her an important life lesson, all of Greek mythology, or the creation stories that are so central to indigenous cultures.

Stories go straight to the heart in ways that information delivered by other means simply can't replicate. When I was studying acting in London, I played guitar and sang at a restaurant on weekends. An elderly couple often ate there, and seemed to enjoy the entertainment. One night, the woman had the waiter hand me a note she'd just written. It read, "Music hurts and heals. You tell the story, and you make it happen." Can you imagine how gratifying that felt?

And how true! The stories that these songs (some of which I'd written) were telling found a way to this woman's emotional center, in a way that I doubt a lecture ever would have done. As speakers, we nearly always focus—and sometimes obsess—on the information we think we need to get across. But there's a world of difference between handing an audience some statistics, and speaking with feeling about why any of it matters to them. In the end, what we're all most interested in is the story of our personal lives. Your job as speaker is to make clear that that's exactly why you're telling this story that impacts each individual listening to you.

Go for the Emotional Impact

Data by itself usually doesn't carry the power to move an audience. However, telling a compelling story that relates those data to human motives—especially to the lives of your listeners—is what delivers the emotional impact you're looking for.

In other words, you need to tap into an audience's emotional responses. As Carmine Gallo says, "If you want to stand out in a sea of mediocre presentations, you must take emotional charge of your audience."[1] Want the scientific side to that argument? "The brain remembers the emotional components of an experience better than any other aspect."[2]

Here's something you must understand to be a speaker who moves audiences: every time you present, you're telling a story. You can call it a 'narrative' if you like. But you're always—or should be—creating a framework so that people can a) make sense of your data, and b) understand that information in terms of how it relates to their own lives and other people's lives. You might be talking about the most technical or conceptual issue imaginable. But if your audience is committed to it in their professional or personal lives, well then, there's usually a huge emotional payout for them in hearing you talk about it.

This is also where drama makes an entrance. Whichever narrative you're delivering will contain peaks and valleys in terms of pacing, intensity, immediacy, conflict, and other inherently dramatic components. And when the people in the story respond to this challenge and take action in the midst of conflict...that's drama! The mere delivery of information in most presentations can't touch this approach in terms of excitement, engagement, and the consuming thought, *"What happens next?"*

That last point is to remind you that you should tell your story in the present tense. Doing so puts listeners right there as the action unfolds. Like this:

> "So here we are, sitting around the conference table, stuck. It's 9:45 A.M. The client is coming at *noon*—and we STILL don't have a design that we think is good enough. We don't have anything that reflects our firm's reputation and leadership, and it's starting to make all of us very nervous. We can see the fear in each other's eyes.
>
> Suddenly, I get an idea. It pops into my head, but I push it right back out. 'That's way too radical,' I think. Then a minute later, I say to myself: 'Wait a minute. What do we have to lose?'
>
> So, I look at everybody, asking myself if I actually have the courage to propose what I'm thinking. Then before I even know I'm going to speak, I'm saying..."

As you can see from this example, stories have a natural forward momentum and drive. If your story is inherently compelling and told well, this forward movement can make the narrative unstoppable. Listeners become intensely interested in the moment-by-moment unfurling of events.

When was the last time you experienced that kind of momentum in a speaker's performance? If you felt it at all, she or he was an excellent storyteller.

A key element of storytelling that makes this happen is the idea of *words as action*, i.e., using language effectively. That means describing incidents that have emotional impact for the listeners themselves and that connects with their personal experiences. Let's go deeper into the ways that storytelling engages and even thrills audiences—young, old, and in-between.

THE RIGHT CHEMISTRY FOR PUBLIC SPEAKING

One reason storytelling is so compelling is because listeners savor experiences that give them emotional pleasure. (Remember how the neurochemical dopamine helps this happen?) That's how your message becomes "sticky" and continues to resonate with listeners long after you've finished speaking. How exactly does this happen? To answer that, let's get our minds around our brains:

The amygdala is in the driver's seat here. It's this part of the limbic system that labels some experiences as significant, perhaps even important for survival. Your audience won't necessarily make that connection consciously. But as long as they sense that they are learning something that is emotionally significant, their brains will be fired up.[3]

This is yet another example of why your brain's anatomy and chemistry are centrally important for speaking skillfully and memorably. Even among brain scientists, the theatrical metaphor is used to suggest how the brain marshals the actions of its different areas of specialty to create a "performance."[4]

You and the Prefrontal Cortex

But now we come to a somewhat delicate situation. We are all members of *Homo sapiens*, which is Latin for "wise or thinking man." That attribute—so critical to our nature as a dominant species—can get in our way when we speak in public!

We are such thinking creatures that it can be hard to turn our powerful brains off to be fully in the moment physically and spiritually. And that is undoubtedly what needs to happen if you're to achieve presence on the public speaking stage.[5]

The executive part of the brain—the prefrontal cortex—controls thought, reasoning, emotion, and planning. As we've seen, this part of the brain is much larger than it is in our closest relative, the chimpanzee.

So how do you use your superior brain to succeed as a speaker? The answer is, you can't let your thinking brain control all the action. You have to give access to your emotional and interpersonal responses. If you focus exclusively on the content you're trying to get across, for instance, you'll be an absentee speaker. You must take in what's happening to you physically and emotionally, as well as noticing how listeners are reacting. If you don't do that, you'll come across as an unengaged speaker, or at least one who's more focused on his or her data than listeners. The result is that you won't have much presence at all.

A convenient way to remember this is that empathy, i.e., the ability to identify with the audiences, is literally embodied. Your brain helps you to find an emotional connection in your story to share with listeners, and your physical response externalizes it for the audience. "You can catch an emotion, just as you can catch a cold," says philosopher Robert M. Gordon.[6] It's one contagion you definitely want your listeners to pick up from you!

And since we're on the subject of the audience's response, consider this: the words and bullet points on your slides activate only the language-processing center of the brain. But stories—with their focus on human psychology and behavior—activate not only the region corresponding to language, but *the visual, sensory, and motor areas of the brain as well*.[7] You might say it's the difference between displaying a black-and-white photo of fall foliage, then switching to one in full color. Simply put, more regions of your audience members' brains "light up" when you're telling them a story.

In Chapter 11, I'll explain how you can employ *stagecraft*—the art of using the stage itself—to strengthen your physical presence. It's one more way to make your stories come vividly to life.

HOW TO TAKE YOUR AUDIENCE ON A JOURNEY

In his 2012 TED Talk, screenwriter and director Andrew Stanton said, "We all love stories. We're born for them. Stories are from who we are. We all want affirmation that our lives have meaning."[8]

Another way to say this is, we recognize *ourselves* in stories. Stories resonate with us because we see ourselves in the events described. We identify with the reactions of the people in the story because we have those same responses. It's the same with your listeners: when they hear a story, their personal beliefs, values, and a lifetime of experiences come into play for them!

Conveying a Story's Essential Meaning

The next step in effective storytelling, is to *convey the story's essential meaning*. The information you convey to audiences as words, facts, and figures is not the essence of what you're getting at. It's incredibly easy to lose sight of this fact when you have a great amount of data to get across.

Listeners have no problem recognizing when you're using data to support your point. A well-told story does something much more powerful, by saying, "This is what this all *means*." Of course, the closer the events of the story are to your audience and their own needs, the more your story will affect them.

If you understand this point, and accept that your audience is the center of everything, it will transform your influence as a public speaker.

A Story Within a Story

When you tell a story well, it's actually a story-within-a-story because it's really about those listening to you. It's actually about *their lives*. Remember, the important people in a room or auditorium are never you and the other presenters—they are the audience. Tell a story well, and the audience members are the one who win in the end. In fact, if you were to create a headline for every one of your stories successfully told, it could read:

*Audience Member Taken on
Transformational Journey, Returns as Hero*

Chris Anderson, curator of TED, says the following about talks that neglect to "frame" a topic well, including taking the audience on a journey:

If a talk fails, it's almost always because the speaker didn't frame it correctly, misjudged the audience's level of interest, or neglected to tell a story. Even if the topic is important, random pontification without narrative is always deeply unsatisfying. There's no progression, and you don't feel that you're learning.[9]

For a skillful demonstration of weaving data into an interesting story, visit TED's own archive and watch Dr. Sandeep Jauhar's talk on "How Your Emotions Change the Shape of Your Heart."

Dr. Jauhar is able to introduce his topic, reveal his main points, and show how they relate to a lay audience, all within a narrative having to do with functional cardiology. It's an impressive feat!

Are You Getting Audiences to Feel?

Compare that to all the speakers that use "soulless PowerPoint slides, facts, figures, and data...while neglecting to engage with audiences emotionally."[10] Equally important, compare it with your own presentations, and always ask yourself if you're using these pro forma tools while leaving out emotional engagement.

As theater professional and trial consultant David Ball reminds us, storytelling goes beyond informing listeners, "to make jurors [in our case, the audience] want to do what you want them to do. This is best achieved by storytelling, because a story influences not only what jurors think, but also what they feel. By influencing what jurors think and feel, you control what they want to do."[11]

After all, if one of your main tasks (and it should be) is to connect emotionally with listeners, why not use the emotion-rich technique of storytelling to do it? As I mentioned earlier, *every* decision involves emotions. You make your own job of creating influence much easier by establishing an emotional connection with the audience before they make any decisions about you and your topic. Stories, in other words, pave your way—smoothly, reliably, and swiftly.

So, don't ever just 'speak.' Create an emotional experience for the audience.

EXPLODE! FLY APART! DISINTEGRATE! — THE TRANSFORMATIONAL MAGIC OF STORYTELLING

What about the "how" part of telling stories as a public speaker? It's easy to discuss what stories *should* do in terms of helping you reach and influence an audience. But how do you actually do it? Let's discuss the practical ways you can transform your performances in speeches and presentations through the magic of storytelling.

Are You Playing It Safe?

First, some questions: Are you playing it safe by making every reference or story about your industry or sector? Or do you explore areas outside your chosen field to discover connections with your work that you can share with audiences? If you're a physician, do you read any philosophy? If you're the general counsel for a tech start-up, are you spending any time with poetry? As an expert in risk analysis for capital projects, are you into astronomy, cooking, or history?

It's all about being engaged with the world and what's happening in it, including what great thinkers have said about it in the past. One of my acting teachers at the drama academy maintained, for example, that 30 percent of our reading should have nothing to do with theater or the stage.

Why? Because as an actor—or small business owner, financial analyst, or CEO who speaks in public—you will be more interesting and insightful if you're aware of other areas of knowledge. And once that happens, you may find you can use an historical reference, a line of poetry, or something else that will enrich or strengthen the point you're making.

I vividly remember, for instance, that after playing Macbeth on stage, I was amazed to see a painting in London's Victorian and Albert Museum of the famous 19th-century actor Edmund Kean in the exact pose (and in an eerily similar costume) that I had used at one point in our company's performance of the play!

But whatever your profession or industry, if you're speaking in public, one realm you should absolutely be exploring is fiction.

Which brings me to Ray Bradbury.

If you don't know Bradbury (1920–2012), I suggest you remedy that situation as quickly as possible. In this American author's thirty-plus novels—but much more so in his nearly 600 short stories—you'll discover a paean to childhood summers, spooky October nights, and an ongoing exploration of the mysterious and the wonderful. But most of all, you'll find the work of someone who loved ordinary people, and shared the values that informed how he thought about and depicted them.

Speak with Zest, Gusto, and *Fun*!

Among Bradbury's works (*Fahrenheit 451, The Illustrated Man, The Martian Chronicles*), is an almost unknown small treasure of nonfiction titled *Zen in the Art of Writing*. In it, you'll find vintage Bradbury in terms of small-town and big-hearted advice about the joy of writing.

For example, here's his view that writing is pure excitement: it's like "thunder, lightning, and wind," that the great authors attempted to grasp with "animal vigor and intellectual vitality."[12]

Zest. Gusto. Love. Fun. These are the guiding stars of the creative process Bradbury is telling us to keep our eyes on. He's saying: *pour* all of your loves and hates into what you write about (for you right now reading this book, that means what you speak about). And simply give yourself over to the passions that result.

Explode! Fly apart! Disintegrate! Those are his words. "Be cool tomorrow," I can almost hear him saying. "As for today…burn down the house!"

Reveal the Passion at the Heart of Your Business

Can this advice make a difference in how you speak to stakeholders? Of course, it can. After all, if you're not passionate about what you do, why should anyone else be? Your passion—and a desire to share it—can create a similar passion in those whose lives you're trying to change for the better.

Therefore, be willing to explode. And here's some practical advice that gets to the heart of this aspect of performance: *Let your passion show regardless of how vulnerable it makes you feel.* Don't worry: all of the vital information in your talk won't go anywhere, and you'll be able to access it just as easily. You'll simply have transformed yourself into a more exciting speaker.

CLOSE-UP

6 Storytelling Tips to Tell a Great Business Story

Do you tell stories with the kind of emotional power that moves audiences? Here are **six business storytelling tips** that will help you engage and even excite listeners. They are the techniques I've taught to CEOs and boards of directors, corporations, United Nations diplomats, government agencies, political candidates, non-profit groups, and TEDx speakers, among others.

You'll notice that these approaches require planning and preparation. That kind of work is necessary for you to get on the right wavelength and connect with the audience.

Common storytelling advice about the hero's journey, archetypes, etc., is fine. But you're better off asking yourself questions about *this* group and how you can reach them than what Jason did in his pursuit of the Golden Fleece. My advice is to start and end with your actual audience's needs and desires. Everything you say from that starting point on the journey will land you on the right shore.

Tip #1 — Find the Interest. Who is this group? What turns them on about this topic? What do they *need?* It's a common mistake to try to "be a great storyteller." That's like attempting to hit the bull's eye without shooting the arrow. In other words, do the work that needs to be done. When you start with the audience's need that you're trying to satisfy, the story tends to write itself.

Tip #2 — "How Can I Weave My Essential Information into a Story?" Instead of dumping a truckload of data, trends, agenda items, and graphs onto your audience, just tell them about a problem someone had. For instance: "I'd like to tell you about a company that was famous for their great products. But all at once, they found themselves in a terrible position. Their products were still first-rate. But their industry changed overnight because of a sudden catastrophe…" Getting interested? Or should I put up the slide with those six bullet points again?

Tip #3 — Build the Story Around Your Audience. You may be tempted to construct your story using a template that an expert says is "one of the seven essential story archetypes," or something similar. Don't do it! Always begin with your audience's needs so you can *tell the story in their terms* from the start. You'll discover events, personalities, trends, industry specifics, or challenges they've actually faced, as well as other elements closely related to their lives.

Tip #4 — Describe Everything in Terms of Human Behavior. Consider how all of the data you want to convey reflects human behavior. Sound like a challenge? It may be. But the idea, once again, is to tie information to people's experiences, needs, and the history of how they acted. For instance, you can mention a fact and leave it at that. Or you can explain the motives behind what happened and how the subsequent events affected people's lives. Now it's human and interesting. And don't be surprised if the drama inherent in a story like that starts to emerge and gets people's pulses racing!

Tip #5 — Use Emotional Language. For audiences to have an emotional response, they must understand the meaning behind the data. To help make that happen, use the language of emotions. "We were pleased with this unexpected outcome," is a bloodless version of: "We couldn't believe what we were seeing!" And don't forget *the power of the pause* to slow things down, to give time for the emotion to be felt, and add drama.

Tip #6 — Add Some Humor (including the self-deprecating kind). Sure, business is a serious affair. But nobody likes to think they're listening to one of the Brothers Grimm just because there's a story being told. Humor lightens the moment; it's entertaining; it makes an audience like you; and it shows that you have a balanced outlook toward the topic. Notice any humorous connections to your story. Savor them, then give your listeners a taste.

CHAPTER 10

The 7 Essential Qualities of Speaking for Leadership

> Be daring, be different, be impractical; be anything that will assert
> integrity of purpose and imaginative vision against the play-it-safers,
> the creatures of the commonplace, the slaves of the ordinary.
>
> —*Cecil Beaton*

Leadership is performance. To be more specific in terms of this book:
leaders speak; and speakers lead.

There's no doubt that when you're delivering a presentation, you
have the starring role, wherever you are in terms of your organization's
hierarchy. It's important, then, that you tap into your natural talents. But
you need to go further. You should also be aware of what I call "The 7
Essential Qualities of Speaking for Leadership."

Together, these qualities lead audiences to trust you. If they do, they
will see you as authentic. The more open and natural you are with audiences, the more you will succeed in influencing them positively.

Speaking as a leader, then, means acting like one.

The 7 Essential Qualities of Speaking for Leadership

Here are the qualities you should exemplify: (1) Integrity, (2) Passion, (3)
Energy, (4) Goodwill, (5) Vulnerability, (6) Empathy, and (7) Humility.

Naturally, your performance skills matter as well whenever you take
center stage. But public speaking is always a journey that the speaker and

audience go on together. Therefore, your effectiveness goes far beyond content and your expertise in other areas. It hinges upon whether the people in the room or auditorium are better off for your having spoken to them.

It's all part of what I call *high-impact speaking.*

What Does It Mean to Speak as a Leader?

Nowhere is the statement written above, 'leadership is performance,' truer than in public speaking. Therefore, if you're a leader in your organization or industry, or you aspire to become one, this chapter is of particular relevance for you. In the drama observed by stakeholders in your company or industry, you will sometimes be center-stage as the "leading man" or "leading lady." In addition, the most successful leaders have an intuitive sense of theater—they perform many roles and convince others to play their parts.

Of course, your performance abilities don't only matter when you're giving a speech. Whenever you interact with others as a leader, you're in the spotlight. People make judgments about you based on the way you speak, sound, move, and interact with the world.

So, are you ready to speak for leadership?

Leadership and Spoken Communication

Speaking as a leader will transform the most important component of your professional success: effective communication. In a survey conducted by the presentation software company Prezi, 70 percent of working Americans agreed that presentation skills are critical to their career success.[1] And a *Harvard Business Review* survey showed that communication and presentation skills are among the C-suite level competencies that companies prize most.[2] Another *HBR* article said it all in the title: "Leadership Is a Conversation."[3]

The good news is that to embody leadership qualities when you speak, your most powerful strategy is a simple one: tapping into your natural talents. Public speaking, that is, reflects who you are. Should any role be easier for you?

One thought that can send you down the wrong path, however, is believing that giving a presentation is something special. It's easy to consider a speech as an out-of-the-ordinary event, a moment of high visibility in which you need to rise above your ordinary competencies. But the truth is, you're always performing! (See Chapter 2, "Why You're a Natural Performer" and my discussion of Erving Goffman's book, *The Presentation of Self in Everyday Life.*)

Let Yourself *Be* Yourself: The sooner you realize that even a high-profile speaking event is just one more performance the more readily you'll let yourself be yourself. That's important because audiences just want the real you. Any attempt to look and sound "excellent" will advertise itself as just that. Listeners truly want to know and to connect with *you*—and allowing that to happen is one of the ways you achieve actual excellence as a speaker.

Still, if you decide you want to reach your own "next level" to speak for leadership, you'll probably have to recalibrate and raise the bar on your personal expectations and level of performance. So here, below, are some ways to grab a winning ticket in the Public Speaking Memorability Sweepstakes.

What's Your Leadership 'Size'?

Your best guide for elevating your performance to the right level is to learn from the actor's art, i.e., to take a page from the stage. I'm speaking of your leadership *size*. Stage actors (as opposed to movie and TV actors) need the ability to project their persona across physical space. Consider this: the distance from the front of the stage to the last row of the orchestra in a Broadway theater may be as much as 150 feet—and much more when balconies are included.

Okay, you're not acting a role and you'll often have a microphone while speaking on a stage. But not always. Acting and public speaking share the need to speak with impact to an audience. So, you must cultivate the ability to reach all members of a large group, not only with your voice but your overall persona. Anything that comes between you and the audience, e.g., a lectern or a considerable distance between you and listeners is a hindrance to achieving that result. In the case of any such obstacle, your performance persona needs to be big enough to prevail.

Ask yourself, then, "What's my leadership size?" Occupying the performance area with energy and confidence, for instance, is a clear mandate of speaking as a leader. *Whatever the message, your physical presence needs to equal or exceed your material.* You can gain size by making your movement and gestures—along with your overall energy—exactly large enough to reach the person farthest from you. (The same is true of your vocal projection.) You need to create just the right size for your speech in terms of the audience *and* venue.

Become Practiced at Presenting Yourself. Whether it's gestures, facial expressions, eye contact, or your use of the stage, you must become practiced presenting not just information, but yourself. You need to be slightly larger than life! Doing so is one way you embrace *every* member of the audience in a venue. Later in this chapter, I'll share some specific techniques of the theater that will empower you to do this in practical performance terms.

Finally, as a leader who speaks you'll be trying to persuade stakeholders from employees to boards to customers and other external audiences. And some of them will be tough crowds. Clearly, this aspect of leadership requires more than great platform skills. It means in part incorporating the specific qualities that are the focus of this chapter. Let's look at each of them.

1. Integrity

Who do you know who speaks with integrity? As you think about your answer, consider whether the person is in the public esteem. If so, that man or woman is a perfect example of someone who achieved ethical leadership at least partly through public speaking. And when the opposite is the case—when someone abuses his position or speaks to manipulate rather than lead—it's just as obvious.

In March 2017, South Korea's Constitutional Court removed President Park Geun-hye from office for corruption. She was accused of helping a friend to secure bribes. Defending herself before the media, President Park called the charges "a fabrication and falsehood," adding, "it's completely framed." Clearly, Korea's high court didn't believe her protestations.

When a person without integrity speaks, we sense immediately that trustworthiness is missing, and we don't believe what the individual says. Think of our own former president, Richard Nixon, who lacked integrity in the eyes of the members of Congress who were about to impeach him and who felt the need to resign before the legislators could act.

Authenticity and Trust: The Building Blocks of Integrity

Ethical speaking is as important as above-board behavior in any other aspect of leadership. Today, trust and credibility can be lost in a moment of thoughtlessness or bias in an interview, in front of an open microphone, or in an ill-considered tweet. Unfortunately, we hear such discourse too often by representatives of some of the institutions that rule our lives. Each of us has the individual obligation, however, to adhere to the standards of our own integrity—including when speaking in high-visibility situations.

I remember clearly the first public speaking workshop I conducted for diplomats at the United Nations in New York. The workshop's sponsor was the United Nations Institute for Training and Research (UNITAR). Prior to the start of the training, in the group's offices across the street from the General Assembly Building where the workshop was being held, I noticed a poster. It showed a hand making a highly recognizable gesture, with the thumb rubbing against the inside of the index finger. Displayed on the poster was the same saying written in at least a dozen languages, most prominently in English:

Bribery is the same in any language.

In terms of authenticity and trust when you give a speech, always ask yourself, "Am I serving my listeners rather than myself in what I'm about to say? And will it be obvious to my audience?" When you speak for leadership, your aim is to change your world, in some way large or small. To do that, you need to be authentic so that people will trust you.

Consider, that *integrity leads to influence.* Listeners who don't trust a speaker will never truly open themselves to that person's influence so their thinking or behavior is changed. To persuade and inspire audiences—to get them to buy into your leadership—you must be whole. That means integrating your personality and values into your performance. To do so is to achieve a form of integrity you absolutely need if you want to be a speaker with genuine presence.

2. Passion

pas·sion n. 1: a powerful emotion or appetite. (*The American Heritage Dictionary, Second College Edition.*) Any powerful or compelling emotion or feeling, as love or hate (dictionary.com).

Great speaking is never about just educating an audience—it's always about creating an experience. For leaders especially, your ultimate success depends partly upon your performance. And that means sharing your passion with listeners.

Think of some of history's most effective speakers when it came to moving audiences. That list includes people like Theodore Roosevelt, Winston Churchill, Sojourner Truth, Martin Luther King, Jr., and today, Malala Yousafzai.

Even if you don't speak at that level, like these speakers you probably have a passion for your topic and want to share it with audiences. Often the problem (as I've mentioned earlier in this book) is externalizing what you're feeling so listeners get it. Audiences aren't mind readers. They must be *shown* your qualities as a leader, including your commitment to an idea. Let's look, then, at how you can get listeners to see and share your passion.

One of the most powerful ways you can do so is by using effective acting techniques. Your goal here isn't to win an Oscar, of course—it's for you to be as passionate a speaker as you can. Actors spend their entire careers learning how, first to access, then to externalize their feelings. Only when they do so will audiences receive the full emotional impact of the moment. As a public speaker, you should master this lesson from the actor's playbook.

Acting Techniques and Public Speaking

David Thomson, a writer on theater and film, published a book titled *Why Acting Matters.* Actor and director Simon Callow discussed the book in a review in *The Wall Street Journal* titled, "The Art of Persuasion." I mention this because it deals with a relevant fact for speakers—that "acting matters" in business and other professional endeavors as well.

In fact, actors and business leaders so often take part in the same activities—engaging, influencing, and moving audiences—that sometimes it's difficult to see daylight between the two. There are differences of course, including the most important one that actors play other people while as a leader you play yourself. But the primacy of the performance in both professions is undeniable.

Your performance itself is the essence of your talk as much as what you speak about. Do you consider that a radical idea? Yet if it isn't true, why are you delivering this speech, presentation, or pitch, or participating in this media interview? You could much more easily email the content to interested parties without having to be present to discuss it!

You therefore need to *act* when you speak, not as a character, but as yourself. What I mean by that is externalizing your passion so an audience sees it, hears it, and feels it. In other words, audiences both need and desire the content to be filtered through you.

You Are the Key. Speaking this way is part of the paradox shared by you and stage actors. While your audience might be the "Be-all and the end-all" (in Macbeth's words), *you are the key* to getting the ideas across. In fact, you are the only one who can give listeners what they need. By definition, that's far more than the content alone can accomplish.

You should aim to be yourself at your passionate best. After all, it's the role of a lifetime!

3. Energy

Here's a secret that will give you a head start over the competition when it comes to influencing audiences:

Public speaking is an exchange of *energy*.

If you enjoy physics, think of this in terms of Sir Isaac Newton's Third Law, which is popularly known as "For every action there is an equal and opposite reaction." In other words, the amount of energy you send toward listeners will be returned to you as increased interest and engagement.

Remember the bubble visualization I discussed earlier? An *invisible bubble* encompasses you, the person farthest from you in the audience, and everyone in between. It's an energy bubble—and everyone inside it feels your power as an energetic and dynamic performer. That's the impression you should give an audience!

It's as though your vitality takes hold of people's imagination and says, "Wait until you hear this!" This concept is important, because any speech that isn't vital in terms of an energized performance will stay firmly tethered to the earth. Don't make your presentations into that kind of talk. As an actor, I strive for performance intensity in every performance, and I do the same as a speaker, whether it's an in-person appearance or a virtual meeting. You should do the same.

The Incredible Shrinking Speaker

Chances are you've never read Richard Matheson's great 1950s sci-fi thriller, *The Shrinking Man* (retitled for the 1957 movie as *The Incredible Shrinking Man*). Here's the plot: while out on his boat, ordinary guy Scott Carey is exposed to a radiation cloud (unfortunately, just after accidently ingesting some insecticide). The strange combination causes him to start *shrinking* at a steady and alarming rate. Soon he's small enough that he must fight for his life against a backyard sparrow, then his own cat. As things get progressively worse and he gets more and more minute, he faces the deadliest enemy of all: a black widow spider!

Sadly (but not nearly as intriguingly), we suffer from the equivalent today in some speeches and presentations. I call this phenomenon THE INCREDIBLE SHRINKING SPEAKER.

Part of the reason we are "smaller" speakers nowadays is that modern life has allowed us to become lazy communicators. In the past, we expressed our whole personalities when we spoke. We had to, because we were forced to use full vocal production and body language. We spoke to people from adjoining fields or backyards, and in public spaces like marketplaces. When indoors, it was lecture halls, factories, general stores, and meeting houses. To get what we were saying across in these spaces, *we had to project our voices and use our bodies.* Yet today, cell phones, cubicles, voice mail—and lately, a pandemic necessitating only virtual presence—have *shrunk* our physical and vocal personas.

Like Scott Carey, we're steadily shrinking! But to speak as a leader, you need to recover some of this power and size. For one thing, people literally look up to you on stage. Your presentations need a higher-octane version of you because that is what audiences expect in a leader.

Below are twelve ways you can *own the room* to speak for leadership. The list should remind you that powerful material combined with a dynamic performance is the winning combination. Become familiar enough with these techniques so that they become your new habits whenever you speak.

CLOSE-UP

Twelve Ways to Speak for Leadership (and Own the Room)

Here are a dozen ways to show whenever you speak that you're the real deal when it comes to speaking for leadership.

1. **Display Confidence and Control:** Confidence in a speaker is self-perpetuating. Listeners will simply be willing to believe what you say if they see that you're confident. That makes it much easier for them to buy into your vision.

2. **Launch Strongly and Conclude Powerfully:** What are the most important moments in your talk? The opening and closing! Your opening especially is like a space launch: it it's successful, the mission has a good chance of succeeding. If it doesn't get off the ground with sufficient power behind it, it all ends right there.

3. **Give Your Audience a Roadmap of Your Talk:** At the start of your talk or presentation, let the audience know where you're going together. Then take them there. Audiences want to feel that they're in good hands. The speaker who lays out a clear path forward is the one who sounds like a leader. Throwing out one data point after another without explaining the road ahead will leave your audience desperate for any landmark.

4. **Move Fluidly and with Purpose:** Learn this essential lesson if you don't already know it: what an audience *sees* of you in action is how they'll judge you. Aim to make yourself the picture of self-assurance, even if you don't always feel that way. And when you gesture, make it clean and emphatic, i.e., let it stand out!

5. **Take Charge of Your Performance Space:** Whenever you speak as a leader, the space you occupy is yours to use. That is to say, you own it. That's true whether you're on a convention stage or standing at a conference table. Don't stand like a monument; and don't wander or pace back and forth like a tiger in a cage. Make your movement purposeful. And that podium? Ignore it and move to center-stage (as long as you have a lapel mic). You'll look fearless and ready for anything.

6. **Speak with the Voice of a Leader:** If a powerful voice isn't one of your assets, get help with it from a speech coach whose background is in theater. Your voice is an essential tool for influencing others. A professor of mine used to say, "If someone's voice is weak, he or she is a weak person." That's not true by a long shot. On the other hand, if your voice doesn't compel people to listen, you're working uphill all the way.

7. **Be Clear and Concise:** Some execs are such high-achievers in their industry that they don't feel the need to prepare for a presentation. "I can talk about this all day long," they think. And unfortunately, it starts to feel like that for their audiences. Therefore, in your own talks, spend some serious prep time shaping what you're going to say so it's clear, concise, and logical. It shows you care.

8. **Tell Stories.** As we saw in Chapter 9 on storytelling, the ability to tell stories is valuable currency for any speaker. That certainly applies to leaders, who are basically telling the story of their organization or constituency. Facts and data inform all right but you need to get to the emotional heart of your message. Stories light the fire of people's imaginations. If you're not *inspiring* followers as a leader, why are you speaking?

9. **Use the Magic of Language:** Conscious use of compelling language can help raise your talks from the mundane to the memorable. Abraham Lincoln knew this as did Winston Churchill. When Hillary Clinton spoke of that "basket of deplorables," she learned this lesson the hard way. Using comparisons, metaphors, and similes can make your message come to life. Just think carefully about using the right language in terms of your objective.

10. **Commit Totally to Your Ideas:** Few things compel attention more than a speaker who believes heart and soul in an idea. A fierce commitment to your message forgives a multitude of sins concerning your platform skills. Play it safe by just sharing data, as many speakers do, and you'll sink without a trace.

11. **Be Conversational.** Public speaking in America used to be part of The Age of Oration. But that era died out sometime between President John F. Kennedy's inaugural speech in 1961 and Bill Clinton's election in 1992. George W. Bush bought the headstone for the burial; Donald Trump wrote the epitaph. Have you learned the lesson that these presidents internalized—that you need to just talk to listeners, no matter how large the group? Remember, each audience member is the same person you might chat with at a coffee shop or the neighborhood diner. Every speech is *conversational* now, no matter how exalted the subject matter.

12. **Physically Express Your Message:** Think of this as your culminating speaking skill. Ask yourself this question: "Now that I have this wonderful content, am I literally embodying my speech in performance?" When you speak as a leader, it's your persona people are buying. Of course, you could always just send a text message. But a speech?…Ah, now you're *talking!*

4. Goodwill

What type of speaker are you?

Too many presenters today are more concerned with their social media followers, book deals, or their next promotion than with the needs of listeners.

Goodwill, on the other hand, means benevolence or concern with the audience's interests. Speakers who demonstrate goodwill are more memorable because they concern themselves first and foremost with their audience's needs. These are people like George Washington, Mahatma Gandhi, Mother Teresa, and Nelson Mandela.

These speakers embodied the behavior that leadership expert John Baldoni in his book *The Leader's Pocket Guide* tells us is necessary. There he advises, "Radiate hope and confidence. Leaders need to give people a reason to believe in themselves."[4]

A Tale of Two Speakers

Speaking like that means fostering a maximum level of *engagement* in listeners. As an example, here's a true story I call "A Tale of Two Speakers…a Universe Apart."

These individuals were keynote speakers at the annual meeting of a professional association I attended. Each was a scientist. The first keynote was ceremonial, while the second was visionary. But that doesn't explain why one speech reached escape velocity while the other never left the launch pad.

What was it that allowed one speaker to be interesting, the other boring? Put simply: one talk was *engaging*, and one wasn't.

It has to do with what I call The Big Bang Theory of Public Speaking. Cosmologists used to believe that everything was steady and unchanging in the universe (a belief system that's actually called the steady-state theory). Nowadays, however, most scientists believe something very different. They believe that the universe began with the "Big Bang," when all matter exploded outward from an unimaginably dense central point. Everything that now exists—galaxies, stars, planets, moons, asteroids, you and me—continues not only to rush away from that central explosion, but does so at ever-increasing speed.

Creating Your Own Big Bang. You have to create your own "big bang" when you present, rather than offering a boring steady state where everything looks and sounds the same. You do so by posing three questions to yourself: (1) "Do I know how to have an interesting conversation with audiences?" (2) "Do I vary the mechanics of my presentation by using slides, questions, video clips, a demonstration, stage movement, etc.?" And most important: (3) "Do I conduct an audience analysis so I know who these people are and what they're likely to expect or prefer?"

Some of the important elements of an audience analysis are obvious: demographics, level of knowledge of the topic, industry experience, etc. Also relevant, however, are culture, preferences concerning how to receive information, and any emotional climate that may exist for these listeners. For instance, have there been recent changes in the company or industry? Has a cherished leader left or passed on recently? Will the issue you'll be talking about present difficult alternatives for listeners? Also, if you can find out who has spoken to this audience in the past. What approach did they use, and was it successful?

> ENGAGEMENT AND LEADERSHIP:
> In a McKinsey study, male and female executives gave "engaging" a score of 4.1 on a 5-point scale as one of the five key capabilities of centered leadership.[5]

By answering these questions, you'll be much better armed as you approach your engagement. You'll then be able to put together content that will *give these listeners exactly what they need to hear on this occasion.*

Remember, engaging an audience and demonstrating goodwill means more than just delivering quality content. It means reaching people—to persuade, inspire, motivate, or activate them. You can hardly accomplish these things if your notes or slides override your concern for the people you're talking to.

CLOSE-UP

20 Ways to Relate to an Audience

1. Get out from behind that lectern!
2. Wear a lapel microphone, and move around.
3. Make solid and real eye contact.
4. Get your body and face into the act!
5. Be conversational.
6. Use humor and self-deprecation.
7. Speak in terms of the audience's needs.
8. Use "you" and "we," not "I" and "me."
9. Ask frequent rhetorical questions.
10. Access the three adult learning styles: visual, auditory, and kinesthetic.
11. Use shared cultural references.

12. Tell stories don't deliver data.

13. Make each main point a distinct segment.

14. Use concrete, specific, vivid language.

15. Speak visually, creating "word pictures."

16. Pause so listeners can take a breath.

17. Get closer to the audience if you can.

18. Speak from notes not a manuscript.

19. Thou shalt not read thy PowerPoint slides!

20. Move naturally, using all the parts of the performance area.

5. Vulnerability

Surprised to see vulnerability as a necessary quality for great speaking? It is, though… and the reason can be explained in just two words: *being yourself.* That seemingly natural attribute can be one of the hardest things to achieve when you're speaking for leadership.

Here's why: for many of us, speaking in public comes with self-consciousness and often anxiety. And that can lead to playing only defense. You might wear an invisible suit of armor that you feel is necessary to protect you from resistance or even hostility. Another common defensive tactic is "trying to be excellent." In both cases, you're headed toward the wrong goalpost. Basically, when you act like this, you're just trying to get through the speech with your skin intact.

But if you want listeners to change in some positive way, they need to trust you. And you can only score points in that game if you're being honest with the audience. Listeners will trust you if they believe they're seeing the real unadorned you—including your vulnerability. Only after that level of trust is established will they be willing to be influenced by you. Like any good performance art, public speaking reflects who you really are and what you're all about.

What You Can Learn from Actors About Vulnerability

As a stage performer, I can attest that, actors demonstrate vulnerability in all kinds of roles.[6] They must open themselves up, again and again, to allow a new personality in. And in the hands of a great playwright or screenwriter, the flaws and weaknesses of these characters will be on full display. Great acting, therefore, is a form of total openness to the demands of a role and the portrayal of a complex human being.

And here's the fascinating result: audiences accept the reality of the person in front of them even though they know it's really an actor playing a role. They are exercising what's called "the willing suspension of disbelief." There's no doubt that there's a paradox here having to do with truth and artifice. But that is the nature of the dramatic art.

The need to gain the trust of an audience through honesty is just as great in public speaking as it is in acting. And one of the challenges for both speaker and actor is to become comfortable being that naked on stage. But here's the thing: *it's because the audience sees your vulnerability that they know they can trust you.* Display something other than honesty—such as consciously trying to be a charismatic speaker—and it will play tinny and false.

Now for the really good news: being honest with an audience is literally effortless. Delivering a speech in a full suit of armor, on the other hand, is awfully hard work.

6. Empathy

Public speakers can often seem larger than life. Part of speaking for leadership, after all, is to help audiences feel that they're part of something greater than themselves. But however powerful you may be on the stage or in the media you can only truly touch listeners through your shared humanity. And to do that, you must first understand their hopes, fears, goals, and dreams. For you, "I feel your pain" can never be just a vote-getting ploy. It must be a credo to live by, and to speak by.

Ordinary speakers deliver content. But you must match information to the needs and desires of others while letting them share your vision. To persuade and inspire you have to engage not only people's minds, but also their hearts. The desire to lead is the desire to serve.

How does that play out in terms of public speaking presence? Just as an actor must understand the intentions of the character, you must be attuned to your *purpose*. Just how do you want to help improve your audience's world? That means not only giving them necessary information, but changing their feelings and actions as well. The speaking version of you as a leader is the one who empathizes with listeners; that will allow you to gain their trust so that those essential changes happen.

Find the Emotional Heart of Your Speech

As we've already seen, your goal should always be to establish an emotional connection with your audience. You won't get very far in achieving the leadership quality we're discussing now—empathy—without once again meeting that word "emotion." Call it the currency of your passion for your topic. Empathy is the instrument that allows you to exchange the strength of your feeling with others. Interestingly, this tool works in both directions: from speaker to audience, and back again.

When you can *demonstrate emotion* as a speaker, two things happen: (1) you reveal the depth of your own feeling; and (2) listeners empathize with that emotion and send it back to you. (Once more, mirror neurons in the brain allow this to take place.)

None of this can happen, of course, if you don't show how you feel. You must, as Shakespeare put it, "wear your heart on your sleeve." Iago in *Othello* characterized that as weakness. But you must recognize it as strength in terms of your ability to motivate, excite, and enthrall audiences. A very real danger is that you'll think all of this is too touchy-feely for the serious world of business and you'll refrain from showing any emotions. But audiences can't share your excitement about an important topic if you don't let them in on the secret!

Let's look at how this is done—as always in this book, in practical terms you can use as a performer. I'll use an example of a contemporary speech that's a powerful demonstration of how to show empathy for an audience.

You may recall my earlier mention of Nancy Boudreaux, who helps prevent financial fraud for the State of Louisiana. In 2012, Nancy was slated to speak at a statewide conference of Louisiana's Emergency Preparedness Association. Nancy's speech concerned scams and frauds that often follow natural disasters. The night before her speech, she realized that there would probably be many people in her audience who came to New Orleans following Hurricane Katrina in 2006 to help with rescue efforts and cleanup.

I'll let Nancy herself tell the rest of the story:

It was a large group of about 125 attendees. The grand ballroom was full, and it was a little intimidating. I decided to conduct a poll, so I asked: "How many people in this room came to New Orleans's aid after Katrina?" As I looked at all the hands that were raised, I was overwhelmed with gratitude. My throat closed and my eyes swelled with tears. I managed to choke out, "Thank you" to each side of the audience.

I was anxious to see my evaluations afterwards… and was stunned at the positive comments! I couldn't help but wonder if anyone had ever thanked them for the sacrifices that they had made to help New Orleans, and was glad that I'd been bold enough to do just that. It was a turning point in my career. I now seek to connect to the hearts of people in my audiences, and not just their minds.

7. Humility

You'll probably find that this particular attribute of speaking for leadership is a balancing act. As a leader, you often need the largest audience possible to hear your message for maximum impact. Once you've found such an audience, however, you must subordinate yourself to its needs. And that means being humble, with a true desire to serve.

In reality, that's a mandate of *all* public speaking.

So why is this trait one of the 7 essential qualities of speaking for leadership? Here's why: when you're recognized as a leader, people will assume that you possess ambition in much greater stores than humility. Even if that's the case, you must display this quality as a dimension of your leadership. To borrow from the title of Roger Ailes's book, *you are the message* when you speak.

Ultimately, your success as a leader depends upon meeting the needs of stakeholders. But you also must be seen as serving something larger than your own interests. And that means being humble. It all comes down to speaking with true professionalism, rather than attending to any self-serving factors.

In other words, when you speak as a leader, you're tasked with attaining a delicate balance of power and humility. It's an essential part of the performance dynamic leaders need. So, one attribute of our ongoing definition of stage presence is demonstrated yet humane competence and confidence. Your confidence is there for all to see. But so must be your concern with others. Learning how to display both is a necessary skill of speaking to lead.

A Speaking Version of Yourself

If you aspire to leadership or are already serving in that role, from today on think in terms of the "speaking version" of you. That's the one who is confident, wholly present, serving listeners, and humble. The combination isn't always easy. But if you want to reach a truly memorable level of speaking, you must get there.

And remember to be interesting! You can judge this for yourself. If you're looking forward to just getting the whole thing over with (without sharing your real feelings with listeners), your audience will want it to be over as quickly as you do.

Here again, you can learn from the actor's art. ***The persona you share with an audience equals everything you offer beyond content.*** That is always an enormous part of your success. In the end, it's the equal to whatever else your audience experiences from you. It's also a more direct route to the influence you're trying to achieve.

Are you ready then to accept the challenge of speaking for leadership? Are you up to the task of helping to change your world?

By now, you probably accept that when it comes to this kind of public address, there's a strong relationship between performance and success. In fact, the more you can connect with audiences rather than remaining in the comfort zone of your content, the more successful you'll be. Display the seven gifts named in this chapter, and you'll be giving listeners not only some*thing* they expect, but some*one* of worth.

Let me share with you a happy ending that demonstrates accepting the challenge of speaking for leadership. One of my clients, a European shipping executive, had previously been accepted into an MBA program. But she had held off accepting the slot because she learned that 40% of her grade would depend on class participation and presentations. She was anxious about speaking in public, even in class.

A few days after she had finished my Fearless Speaking coaching course in Boston and flown home, she called me. She wanted to share the news that she had just formally accepted her place in the incoming MBA class. She felt that she now had the confidence to begin the program and perform (in this case speak) well in it.

"I'm so glad I did it!" she said over the phone.

You can imagine how delighted I was to hear this news.

So, start your own journey today toward speaking with greater confidence and influence. And keep this in mind: the more you enjoy yourself, the more your audience will too. That's in addition to their benefitting from your growing presence and audience awareness as a speaker.

CHAPTER 11

5 Powerful Ways to Command a Stage

All power is a trust; that we are accountable for its exercise; that, from the people, and for the people, all springs, and all must exist.

—*Benjamin Disraeli*

By this point in *Speak for Leadership*, you've learned specific approaches, tools, and methods for influencing audiences. You should also have a thorough grounding in three main areas of speaking with impact: (1) the essence of stage presence, (2) accessing your natural talents to exhibit this quality, and (3) using a performance-based approach to public speaking.

Such an approach (as you know by now) means it is vital that you use your instrument—your body and voice—in performance. You understand that you should tell meaningful stories rather than just deliver information. And you realize that an emotional connection with both your material and your audience is necessary. Performances incorporating this mindset will ensure that you speak with true vision and leadership in your business or profession.

At this stage, then, you're primed to be a rare type of speaker. That's the one who excels at the true task of public speaking: to serve the audience rather than oneself or one's material, and to help people change their world.

To excel fully in the *oral arena*, you need just one more component. You must know how to command a stage. That's the subject of this chapter.

I'll be discussing five ways you can command a stage. They work for large or small stages, and in any speaking situation. We've looked at two of them to some extent earlier in this book. Each, however, has importance for this chapter as well.

The remaining approaches come straight from the world of the theater. I've always felt that actors are the best communicators in the world when it comes to moving audiences. Since they train their entire professional lives to accomplish this, it isn't a surprise.

You can use their particular set of skills to command *your* stage. Doing so will give you maximum impact on stakeholders.

FIVE POWERFUL WAYS TO COMMAND A STAGE

One fact should be abundantly clear by now: speaking with presence goes far beyond the mere delivery of content. In fact, that's only your starting point. A world of influence is open to you. But the door will stay closed if you only toss out information from behind a lectern or clicker.

Here's how to proceed instead: once the content of your talk is clear in your mind, start thinking about how you can give a performance that's bold and *interesting*. Pay attention to the five areas I discuss below: body language, voice, facial expressions, stage directions, and connecting with the audience.

1. Body Language

In Chapter 7 of this book, I labeled body language as "the art of physical expression." I focused on why the language of the body is central to public speaking, and why you must incorporate it into your stage persona. I also discussed the biological basis of performance. And I introduced the concept of aligning your physical expression with three things: the venue, the audience's needs, and the moment. It comes down to externalizing what you feel, just as actors do, so the audience can see it.

What I want to talk about now is achieving the *freedom* and *spontaneity* you need to command the stage physically. Accomplish that, and you'll literally be in the position to lead any audience. You'll remove the ever-frequent gap between what you're saying and how powerfully you can express it to others visually and emotionally as well as intellectually.

Creating the Conditions for a Gesture

Would you like to know the question that speech coaches hear more than any other? It's "What should I do with my hands?" But as we know by now, body language goes beyond gestures to encompass the full physical expression of what you're saying. In the world of public speaking performance, words and ideas have physical reality. It's your duty to make it show!

There is a real need for a physical component to what you're saying. When people say, "I can't talk without moving my hands!" they're really acknowledging this unity of thought and bodily expression. It's one of the elements you need to tap into to make your speeches exciting.

If your body is one of your primary tools of communication, how then do you *free it* to make the magic happen? First, keep in mind that you should never have to think about body language. When you're fully invested in what you're saying, your body will respond naturally and organically. And the audience shouldn't particularly notice what is happening physically. If they are paying close attention to the points you're making, your movements and gestures to support those points will be equally effective and not noticeable by themselves.

Here's a prescription I mentioned previously in the chapter on body language that you should fill to make that happen:

**Create the conditions for the gesture
rather than the gesture itself.**

What does that mean? If you are psychologically "primed" to express yourself with passion and commitment, then the gesture that arises at that moment will be appropriate, spontaneous, and honest. Interestingly, the gesture you use while making a point might easily be different each time you give that presentation! There's an enormous difference between gesturing spontaneously and planning a movement for a desired effect.[1]

Two last suggestions: Stay loose and relaxed, as a tense body will reveal itself in stiff gestures. Also, think of gestures as starting from the center of your body, which is your core from which all your strength emanates.

And don't forget to smile.

2. Voice

I spoke earlier about how your voice has the power to transform your relationship with the audience. The voice is unsurpassed in this ability. That's true because of a basic and indisputable fact: it is the instrument *par excellence* for expressing your feelings in performance. Other aspects of the voice discussed earlier in this book include breathing the right way to aid projection; the five key tools of vocal dynamics; and the ways in which the sounds of the words you choose effect how listeners hear and respond to you.

Now I'd like to get a little more intimate concerning using your voice. I want to discuss how you can create a sound that's confident, warm, accessible, and pleasant, yet possesses authority. What I mean is, the type of voice that both seduces and compels others to listen.

Why Your Speech Rate Is Important

First, I'd like you to slow down. It's so easy to get wrapped up in delivering information—often, a lot of information—that you can veer right off the track of fostering audience comprehension! For instance, I almost never have to say to a client I'm coaching, "Could you speed things up a bit?" Between the adrenaline rush of appearing before an audience, and making sure you get all the information in, your delivery can proceed like a runaway freight train.

Always remember that audiences must absorb information in real time. They can't flip the pages back to an earlier portion of a report or business plan to remind themselves of critical data. That's why it becomes your job to *lead them* through your narrative. That means giving them bite-sized pieces of information that they can chew and digest (the food metaphor works well) before you offer them the next mouthful. A pizza comes in eight slices, right? We never say to anyone, "Here . . . eat this entire thing in one bite!"

You therefore need to take the audience on the journey one moderate step at a time. Doing so takes care of two things: it allows listeners to have confidence in your ability to lead; and it helps make your material accessible to them. When you proceed at a pace that's comfortable for you and for them, it's a clear signal that you're a confident speaker. Presenters who seem hurried or nervous just make audiences anxious.

Breathing, Pace, and Fullness of Sound

Controlling your vocal delivery in this fashion begins with the same tool you use to create a well-supported sound in the first place: diaphragmatic or belly breathing. The glottis or opening in the larynx needs to be open when you inhale. But it closes as the vocal cords rub together to create vocal sound. So, if you breathe in a normal rhythm, you'll keep the glottis open with each inhalation preventing yourself from continuing on literally without taking a breath!

Getting a full reservoir of air also leads to a warmer, more resonant and fuller sound. Try this experiment to hear what I mean: First, expel almost all of the air in your lungs. Now say something to an imaginary audience of twenty to thirty people in front of you. Your voice sounds thin and doesn't carry much authority, right? This time, fill your lungs fully before speaking. Doesn't your voice suddenly carry more heft concerning whatever it is you're saying?

The procedure then is, slow down, breathe using the diaphragm for a warm full sound, and take the time to just talk to the audience. Remember, you want to sound as conversational as you do when you're talking with friends. Now you're both gaining control, and creating an authoritative yet friendly voice.

A last word: don't ever worry that your voice isn't "good enough." If you try to change your vocal delivery to sound like a professional speaker or radio announcer, you'll only reduce your honesty with the audience. That's a cardinal sin of any public speaking.

3. Facial Expressions

When it comes to speaking with presence, what you show facially is a vital clue to what you're thinking and feeling. And people will naturally respond to what they're seeing. (I won't spend any time here on detecting deceit through facial expressions. I'm assuming you want to honestly share what you know with audiences.)

As a culture, we tend to discount facial expressions as an element of body language. But human beings get an enormous amount of information based on what the face is showing and the look in someone's eyes. Sometimes, we make life or death decisions based on what we're seeing!

There are forty-three muscles in the face. That's a lot of real estate, and it's there for a reason. You may have heard that it takes more muscles to frown than it does to smile. I've looked into that claim and I haven't found any evidence that that's the case. But human beings tend to smile more than they frown. That means the muscles involved in a smile are probably stronger, which means that it takes more work to frown. I don't know about you, but I don't want to expend a lot of effort doing something that's going to make me and others around me feel bad!

So, is your face expressive? It's a trait you should know about yourself by now. And here's something to remember about facial expressions and the emotions they elicit, both in you and audiences: it works both ways. We know, for example, that when we feel an emotion, we tend to express it physically (when we're happy we smile, when we're sad we cry, etc.). But the reverse occurs as well, because the mind and body recognize each other's states. If you make a sad face, in other words, you'll feel sadder. This means that *by assuming a physical pose you can elicit the emotional response associated with it.*

Doesn't it stand to reason then, that the facial expressions you display will lead your audience to feel those emotions too? (Remember those mirror neurons!) A lack of facial expressiveness, on the other hand, is a disservice to an audience. It deprives people of clues to understand how you feel; how deeply you're committed to what you're saying; and often, how urgent it is in terms of any action needed.

If you know that you don't use a lot of facial expressions, try to incorporate them more into your speaking. It will help foster the emotional connection you should be seeking. Try standing in front of a mirror and giving your speech exactly as you would in front of an audience—actually "saying" the words but without any sound coming out of your mouth. Is your face an accurate indicator of how you feel about your topic?

4. Stage Directions

The fourth way to command a stage isn't on the radar of most speakers. This is using the stage itself as a tool of communication. Where you stand, and where and when you move have a part to play in terms of how powerfully you come across to an audience. In other words, you should use the stage strategically when you speak.

Are you doing that now? When I say "stage," I don't only mean a traditional raised platform in an auditorium. Your stage is whatever space you're speaking in. It may only be six square feet at the end of a board table in a conference room. However expansive or limited the area is, you should use it effectively in performance.

The key to doing so is incorporating the stage directions that actors use.

Take a look at Figure 11-1, below, which indicates this method of charting out a stage. Notice that stage directions are always indicated from the actor's point of view. So, "right" means the actor's right (the left side of the stage as you are looking at it from the audience), and vice versa. Since many stages are raked or tilted slightly upward to aid an audience's view of the performers, "upstage" means toward the back wall, and "downstage" means closer to the audience.

Actors and directors use these designations to rehearse and compose the visual elements of a stage play. A director blocking out a scene in rehearsal will say to an actor, "Cross *up-left* to the table just before you say the line," and the actor understands that that means "Upstage Left," and moves in that direction.

Now, looking at this diagram: which location on stage do you think is the strongest one for you as a speaker to occupy for maximum effect? It's Downstage, and specifically Downstage Center because that's where you are closest to your audience while occupying center-stage.

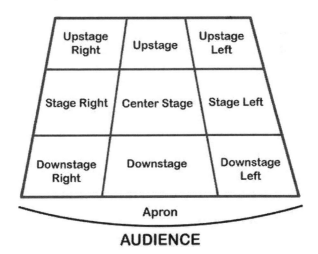

FIGURE 11-1. Stage Directions

Now, which parts of your speech usually have the most impact? It's your introduction and conclusion. Since that's the case, where should you be standing when you deliver them? That's right: downstage-center—whatever that means in terms of the actual space you're occupying when you speak.

I advocate using a different part of the performance space for each segment of your talk. That is, if you stand in one specific spot as you deliver each main point, the audience will associate what you're saying with what they're seeing. That helps each portion of your talk stand out from the others while making it easier for listeners to retain. It doesn't matter which parts of the performance area you use, apart from your intro and conclusion which should be delivered DC. Just remember not to distance yourself from the audience at any moment by standing too far upstage (too far away from the conference table, etc.).

Here's the winning formula for using stagecraft in public speaking: *move to a specific part of the stage and stay there to deliver that mini-section of your speech.* Gesture naturally, but don't move to a different place until the next segment comes up.

Positioning yourself like this in a performance space has two advantages. First, audiences have some visual variety. But even more important, they associate where you stood with what you said when you discussed a point. So not only is it easier for them to be engaged because of what they're hearing *and* seeing unfold in front of them, but afterwards they will recall the "story" you told at each moment of your journey around the stage.

George Washington, Actor

How effective is using the actor's art in a speech? Here's an example from arguably our country's greatest leader.

At the end of the Revolutionary War in March 1783, the Continental Army's officers were angry at rumors that they wouldn't be paid their salaries and pensions. Insurrection against the civilian government was in the air. Commander-in-Chief General George Washington met with the officers and gave a conventional speech urging restraint, which wasn't particularly well received.

He then produced and read out loud a letter he'd received from Congress. He began by squinting at the small writing. Then he stopped speaking, and reached into his pocket. The officers were shocked by what they saw next: the fifty-one-year-old general had taken out reading glasses! Then he said to the officers before returning to the letter:

"Gentlemen, you will permit me to put on my spectacles, for I have not only grown gray but almost blind in the service of my country."

At that moment Washington's officers discovered they were shamed and at the same time filled with affection for this man who had led them through so much. Washington finished reading the letter, then left without saying another word. There was no need for him to remain; and he must have guessed the sentiments in the room. And indeed, the officers immediately cast a unanimous vote agreeing to the rule of Congress. The civilian government was preserved, and the experiment with democracy in America continued.[2]

That's the art of spoken performance on stage.

5. Connecting with the Audience

I've saved the easiest one of the five ways to command a stage until last, so you can start using it right away. It's a skill that should boost your confidence while making you a more dynamic speaker. The skill is *connecting with your audience*. Think of it as "The Three C's": connecting with the audience for greater confidence and comfort.

To explain this essential element of commanding a stage, I need you to step into my time machine. We're going back around 2,800 years, to 800 B.C.

Something significant happened in Western civilization at that time in terms of how we communicate.[3] It was the change from the world of *orality* that had existed up until that time, to the beginnings of *literacy*. After all, Homer's *Iliad* and *Odyssey* were originally epic poems that were spoken and sung in performance, and not written down at all.

Nowadays, you and I swim happily in this literary world. We're completely comfortable reading books, newspapers, and magazines; and writing memos, annual reports, emails, text messages, and all the rest. We include in our efforts, of course, notes and bulleted slides we prepare for speeches and presentations. All very *literary*.

The Oral Arena

But when you speak in public, you're entering what I referred to in Chapter 2 as "the oral arena." And your job now is to perform effectively in that environment. It happens to be a completely different world from the literary domain.

You can be the world's foremost authority on your topic, that is— but your task now is to *share who and what you are.* Yet too many people spend all of their preparation time gathering and polishing their materials (i.e., reading, researching, and writing), and then relating to all of that while presenting. By doing so, they're ignoring the actual role they're being called upon to fulfill before an audience: to verbally, vocally, and visually take listeners on a journey, in real time.

People Over Content: Here's an actor's suggestion if you want to own a public speaking stage: spend less time on your content, and more time getting comfortable in front of people and interacting with them. That means everyone, from your office team to the audience at a national convention there for your keynote. Become practiced at engaging every type of audience you face—and enjoying the hell out of doing so. The truth is, you already have content coming out of your ears. Ease up on spending more and more time on it. Chances are you're weak on the other side of the ledger, i.e., performing your true role in the oral arena. (Hint: You're not there just to deliver information.)

Anyone can read from a spreadsheet or slides. *But your performance is what you give the world.* How you handle the speaking moment determines whether you speak with presence or not. That means making sure that people get what you're saying, understand what you mean by it, and have a strong sense of how you feel about it.

It also means moving and speaking with certainty and a sense of purpose. The content of your speech is good at putting a fence around your topic. But it can't take your audience out of the corral and on the journey you should take together. That's the essence of public speaking, and that's how you can become an effective and fearless speaker.

There is simply no other way to get it right.

CHAPTER 12

Speaking with Presence in Video Conferences

I never saw it coming.

—Professor Zoom

I'm getting to know people. It's not face-to-face, but we'll come back with a new understanding of each other.

—Patricia Kuhl

It's a virtual world now. As I write this, the Covid-19 pandemic has had all of us hunkered down for a second year, in still too many cases with only a digital lifeline connecting us to the rest of the world to conduct business and reach other people.

Or so it seems.

It won't last, of course. And even now amid the fear, the tragic loss of loved ones, and widespread economic damage, we're surviving, learning, and even innovating. And fortunately, talking to colleagues, customers, and clients is easy via our present technology.

There's even more hope than that. Would you believe that all of those online meetings may be helping you to develop a stronger presence when you speak? Let's look at a striking paradox that's literally staring us in the face these days: remote communication is making us more intimate with those we're trying to influence.

189

FACE-TO-FACE COMMUNICATION: STILL THE BEST WAY!

It's actually part of another paradox that applies to public speaking. This one is shared with the other world I inhabit: the theatrical stage. It's this: to have a relationship with a group of people, you have to appear to be talking to everyone individually.

Watch a newsreel of someone on the public speaking circuit in the late nineteenth- or early twentieth- century and you'll see exactly what I mean because of the absence of that sense of individual communication. We've gone from that bombastic style of speaking in public to one that is now expected to be intimate.

In other words, it's all about face-to-face communication now. To connect with hundreds or even thousands of strangers, we are all expected to achieve an outward ease while seeming to just chat with each individual in front of us. Watch speakers who are really good at this and you'll probably get the sense that this is what good public speaking is all about. Talking to audiences with that level of naturalness is hard for most business speakers to grasp—and even harder for them to implement.

This is where Zoom and the other video conferencing platforms come into their own. When you speak into your webcam, it's literally face-to-face. This means you no longer have to pull off the trick of very-public-yet-seemingly-close-up-speaking that you must accomplish on a stage. You *are* close where the camera and digital connection are concerned. Provided you open up enough emotionally, every person attending via video experiences your personality at point-blank range. That automatically lends you a stronger and more immediate presence.

To Be Influential, Be Conversational

Online meetings then are providing you with a powerful if often unrecognized tool. It's the capability—the insistence really—that you be conversational.

Nearly every successful speech these days sounds like the speaker is *just talking* to us. Online presentations haven't changed that. In fact, the person-to-person chat we prefer can be easier to accomplish via a video conference than on a stage. Here's why:

One of the biggest challenges in live talks is something actors spend their whole professional lives learning how to do well: externalizing emotions. I mean the kinds that arise when we're honestly expressing our feelings. As a poet once said, "An actor can break your heart at fifty feet."

But business people often have a hard time making that happen on the public speaking stage. That's not surprising, since they haven't had training in theatrical performance. But your computer and webcam now make it much easier for you. It's not fifty feet anymore; it's two feet. Your part of the conversation can be natural—without the need to project it across space—because we're virtually sitting right here in front of you.

You may in fact have a *better* chance of sharing an emotional connection with us than if you were speaking to us from a big stage. It's precisely that human touch that can help give you a stronger presence in online meetings.

So, let those emotions show, and don't hold back from being intimate. The more you can make it feel like a close and friendly chat, the more *present* you'll be for us.

Why Your Video Conferencing Skills Matter Now

There's another reason why you need to improve your virtual speaking skills *right now*: the world of business communication has changed. However long the Covid-19 pandemic lasts, we won't be going back completely to in-person sales pitches, team meetings, presentations, and strategy sessions. Too many businesses now understand the advantages of online meetings and updates. Large companies especially get it: video meetings make it convenient and cheap to bring together people who may literally be all over the world. The impact on travel budgets alone is monumental.

This development is of obvious importance to those of us giving presentations, making pitches, and otherwise doing business in virtual settings. The percentage of how much of our work falls into that category is only going to grow.

If you need another reason to improve your online speaking abilities, here it is: the virtual "you" is what video conference attendees actually see and hear. Any time you spend on practicing speaking via video will be directly reflected in your real performance. It's no longer a question of practicing *here* to present *there*. Rehearsing in your home or office never had that advantage before, since you'd always be presenting someplace different. Therefore, the question becomes: Are you ready to communicate at your best through the screen persona that may reflect, literally, where you live?

Below are four ways to make an outstanding entrance in the Theater of Virtual Presence, where the curtain has already risen.

HOW TO SPEAK DYNAMICALLY IN VIDEO CONFERENCES

The Camera Is Your Audience. Speak to Them!

The audience watching and listening to you in a video conference is a captive one. And that, as they say, is a good thing. A viewer can only be in one place; and it's your job to direct that person's gaze to the one place *you're* in.

The following analogy of theater vs. film helps explains this: When you sit watching a play, you can look wherever you like in order to observe what's going on in front of you. You can watch the actor who is speaking; but you could look instead at the other actors and *their* reactions. You can admire the scenic design; you can even look up at the lights hung above the stage. When you watch a film, however, your gaze is captive. You can only observe what the camera *wants* you to see since it directs your gaze at all times.

Transfer that thought to video conferencing and it should be clear that when you're speaking, you have to direct every viewer's gaze to *you*. Participating in a video meeting should make every participant's gaze captive to what is on the screen. It's the job of the person speaking to make sure that happens. Virtual meetings are notorious, however, for being filled with opportunities for distractions. If people indulge themselves, you won't even be aware of it.

How to Influence Your Audience Virtually. Therefore, if you want to influence your audience in a virtual meeting, *you must look at the camera because the camera is your viewer's gaze.* The webcam IS the viewer. He or she has to feel that you yourself are not distracted but are making great eye contract so that communication takes place.

Devoting your attention to the webcam like this can take some getting used to. In a telepresence training session that I conducted a few years ago, for instance, the client, located in another room, never seemed to look at his audience (me) once! He always appeared to be glancing over to the side. The reason was that he was looking at me on a monitor. When we watched the recording, it was immediately obvious that he was looking in the wrong place. In effect, I was the webcam, and he never spoke "to me" at all.

Get your gaze right, and you'll come through as present and personal. In our second taping, the change on my client's part was positive and dramatic.

Keep Thy Hands Away from Thy Face!

As you will know if you've ever been interviewed on a talk show, or have spoken with people who sit too close to their webcam, the camera magnifies everything. When you're in a video conference (or any time you're in a close-up), just allowing your gaze to drift to either side can make you look shifty.

It is essential to keep your gaze steady and true! A special precaution: If you're too dependent on written notes, you'll be looking away from the viewer (the camera) too often so that you'll make no emotional connection.

Another unconscious habit that can work against you in a virtual setting is touching your face. Again, the static nature of the camera's eye makes anything that takes place in its limited visual field noticeable. Touching your face looks fidgety and is likely to pull our attention away from what you're saying. Think of it as one of those things you do when you're alone that you wouldn't want others to see. Though you may be the only person in your home office during a video call, you're absolutely not alone!

Body Language Applies to Your Top Half Too

What about those hands? Since you may feel like someone glued to a chair with the camera's eye scrutinizing your every move, won't moving your hands be distracting as well?

Actually, it won't. Body language doesn't only apply to your bottom half after all. Using natural, strong gestures to support what you're saying is just as important if you're sitting down. In fact, people in online meetings who sit stiffly as though they're afraid to move are uncomfortable to watch.

So, feel free to gesture naturally. Just be sure the *size* of the gesture is appropriate. For instance, try to keep it within the width of your body, so your hands and arms aren't flailing outward.

Gestures made the right way look controlled and necessary. They give the impression that *you* are in control.

How to Personalize a Webcam

Perhaps the most challenging aspect of speaking virtually is *personalizing* your webcam. Like everyone, you're at your best when you speak to another human being, not to a recording instrument. Anyway, the whole idea of a teleconference is that your presence reaches everyone, not just the fact that the transmission is working properly.

But speaking remotely often means you're alone in your office, den, or recording studio with literally no one present except a webcam or video camera. (In a recording studio, also present will be at least one camera operator, sound person, director, etc., but they're technical personnel who are only concerned with the production aspects of the shoot.)

Making the Camera Human. How do you project the essence of your personality to a cold recording instrument? You can't. Instead, you have to make it *human*. Here's how.

Imagine that the camera is someone whose opinion you care deeply about. It can be a colleague, mentor, spouse, parent, child, sibling, best friend, or your wise Auntie Jo. Make it someone that you'd like to hear say at the end of your remarks: "Meghan, that was amazing. You really got to the heart of the issue. That's the person I admire. I'm proud of you."

We all want to come across at our very best for someone like that in our lives. You must believe that your webcam is that person watching and listening to what you say. You may be surprised at how this simple visualization can improve your online persona. You owe it to your cyberspace audience (and yourself) to make sure that's the person speaking.

A FINAL THOUGHT ABOUT SPEAKING ONLINE

Recently, I read the following opinion concerning communicating via video conference: that doing so is "somewhere between absence and presence." This is nonsense. Why would you need to be present while speaking online any less than you do in person?

The main difference between the two is that one is electronically transmitted. Other than that, you still need the presence that comes from authenticity. It may not be stage presence. Let's call it instead *video presence*.

Can you acquire this type of presence? Of course, you can. In addition to getting better the more you participate in online meetings, you have a convenient tool available in online coaching and training to help improve your skills. And there's no denying the excitement of influencing people *all over the world* to spur you on to greater accomplishments.

Achieving Intimacy. You only need to adjust your view slightly in order to be a strong presence in video meetings. Consider, as I mentioned earlier that most of the time you're very close to your screen—and so is everybody else. This is a form of intimacy. Whatever distractions that may exist—a child or a barking dog in the background—just reveal another aspect of the person you're talking to (and of you too). If you think about it this way, it's a reminder that this is an opportunity to literally get close to a person that you might not have otherwise.

I won't even mention how comfortable it is to be wearing your pajama bottoms with no one the wiser!

Are You Human Enough? (How to Make Any Audience Love You)

Most people see the problem of love primarily as that of *being loved,* rather than that of *loving,* of one's capacity to love.

—*Erich Fromm*

The realm of public speaking is a domain that demands the best you have to give. The opportunities for creating influence are vast. And like any effort of a lifetime, it's an ongoing and rewarding adventure.

A few years ago, a client expressed this thought better than I ever have. He was the Deputy Permanent Representative, i.e., deputy ambassador, of the Permanent Mission of Sudan to the United Nations. The occasion was the graduation of a two-day "Public Speaking for Diplomats" course I had just conducted at the Mission's headquarters in New York. As diplomats will, the Deputy Representative gave a short speech to honor the occasion. In it, he said this:

"Doctor, when we first invited you here to work with us, I thought you would merely be giving us some pointers for when we get up to speak. But I know now that there is an ocean of influence to be gained from public speaking—and over the last two days, we have waded in only up to our knees."

"Perfect!" I thought.—An *ocean* of influence.

The Challenges You Face. When you speak, you face many obstacles in your quest to make a difference in people's lives. You must corral everyone's attention away from their personal concerns. You have to *entice* them to listen to you and accept what you're saying. And you must make a big enough impression so that your message sticks. If your speech or presentation is especially important, you're pursuing an even loftier goal: *to get your audience to take some action long after you've finished speaking.*

Now that you've finished this book, you're well-armed with the theories and practices for achieving leadership presence in public speaking. It will happen, provided that you stay *human enough.*

Another story, this one from just a few months ago:

The CEO who enrolled in our Executive Speech Coaching Course was a passionate environmentalist. So much so, in fact, that he was the founder of a nonprofit focused on combatting global warming.

But he had a problem. He wasn't coming across as particularly human.

I'm exaggerating…a little. What I really mean—and you've probably seen it yourself—is that even when speaking of his passion, he didn't seem to particularly care about what he was saying. You may ask: "Is that even possible with someone who does care and wants to communicate what he believes to others?" Consider the stresses of the high-profile public speaking pressure cooker, and you'll realize that this disconnect is not only possible, but is actually fairly common.

Always bear in mind that when you speak, you are revealing your thoughts and emotions *through your performance.* To the audience, your speaking persona is simply who you are. The fact that your message is elegantly expressed in your speaking notes or slide deck doesn't matter. If you don't look and sound like you mean it when you say it, listeners simply won't be on the wavelength you think they're on.

That was exactly what was happening with the passionate-though-unconvincing CEO.

You know by now that it's never enough in public speaking to simply share information. Your job is to *change lives,* in ways large and small. Audiences don't need to merely accept you—they need to believe in you. There's no other way to truly get them to open up and be willing to be changed by you.

Whether you're pitching business or delivering a keynote, listeners are buying you as much as your message. We could even say that they need to not only love what you're saying—they must also love *you.* Here are four ways to make that happen.

1. Let the Audience See That You Are Interesting.

Avoid the mistake of playing it safe. A major reason most presentations sink without a trace is that the speaker is intentionally doing exactly what everybody else has done. Here's the thinking that I believe goes along with this mindset: "This type of presentation [lecture] [pitch] [keynote] is always done this way in this situation, so I should do the same thing."

That may seem to you to make sense.

But it really doesn't. For instance, take people who need to overcome their fear of public speaking. In almost every case, speakers with stage fright *try to defend themselves when they're on stage.* Instead of striking out to be visible and interesting, they basically try to get off stage as quickly and invisibly as possible with their skin intact.

Talk about only playing defense! But don't you want to be recognized and applauded? That will never happen if you try to look and sound like every other presenter who's played this venue.

Let's face it: few things are as revealing about who you really are than standing in front of an audience—just you—sharing something that's dear to your heart. Being willing to show your true self in all of your vulnerability is the only way to get an audience to trust who they're seeing. That's the "you" that's unique and therefore interesting—in fact, it's the one they came to hear! Don't play it so safe that you vanish, right there in front of everyone's eyes.

2. Pay Attention to the Care and Feeding of Listeners.

Here's the perfect way not to be upstaged by your data while making the audience comfortable: Feed listeners information in bite-sized pieces.

Again, most presenters don't consider the audience enough when it comes to reaching and engaging them. In particular, they don't consider the differences between written and spoken information. Listeners can only absorb so much in the time it takes for them *to hear and process what you say before you go on to your next point.* You have to make it easy for them. People will process more information in real time if it's presented to them at the right pace!

How can you be sure you're doing that? Think of your speech as consisting of separate segments (most of the time this will be easy to determine from your main points). Each of those segments is a *mini-talk*, interesting and absorbable by itself. The metaphor I use with clients is a pearl necklace: each orb is beautiful by itself, but strung together they equal something incomparable.

Simply signal to the audience that you're moving on to the next segment. This allows them to respond mentally this way: "Ah, that's obviously the end of that idea. Got it. What's next?"

Helping Your Audience Stay with You. You can create this response by doing three things: (1) pausing, (2) using a verbal transition, and (3) inflecting your voice upward as you start the next idea, i.e., raising your pitch. The pause alerts the audience that something different is coming. Your verbal transition gives them time to absorb and "store" your last point while also making it clear that you're about to start a new portion of your talk. And inflecting your voice upward clearly says, "Now here's the something NEW." New ideas *always* prime listeners to prick up their ears.

Without these signals, all the segments of your speech will sound alike, no matter that there is different data in each section. Your talk will come across as one long presentation without any changes of idea. To listeners, the information will simply be piling up. They will feel like they don't have time to take a mental break and absorb anything!

3. Your Story Really Needs to Be All About Your Audience.

As you've read elsewhere in this book, emotion—not data—is the currency that makes you likable and memorable for audiences. While the information you impart may be essential for an audience to know, your lasting impact resides in how you make them feel.

Here again, too many presenters misread the drama of public speaking by casting themselves in the role of messenger. But that's only a starring role in the ancient Greek tragedies of Aeschylus, Sophocles, and Euripides and the other tragedians whose plays are now lost to us. (In stage tragedies during the Golden Age of Athens, violence always occurred offstage, and a messenger described the momentous events. The part of messenger, though small in terms of lines spoken, was really a starring role.)

Today, however, merely delivering data makes you anything but a star! If stuffing information into people's heads were all that mattered, why wouldn't you just email your report or deck? Why would anyone invite you to speak at a live or virtual event? Your content does its job quite adequately. But you have a different part to play.

Think of it this way: your job isn't to deliver the goods. It's to create the good. As we've seen, that requires an emotional connection; and usually, storytelling. What I mean isn't necessarily telling actual stories; it's delivering your information as a story—one that's ultimately all about your audience. When you think of your content in these terms—not of information delivered but as your means for improving people's lives—your approach to speaking can and should undergo a sea change.

Delivering Your Data in Narrative Form

It will be easier to do this if you understand that every presentation is a narrative of some kind. Your job is to weave your data into that story so that it's human and interesting. And this part is essential: to make your story as powerful as possible, *always frame it within the context of your audience's needs and desires.* Talk about actual people; seek out real examples from your company, society, etc.—whatever serves your purpose in making the story come alive for THIS audience. Ultimately any story you tell should be about these listeners. It makes perfect sense: the more the audience can identify the elements of your story with their own lives, the more they will like what you're saying and take it to heart.

Also, look for ways to give pertinent information that educates your audience, including the story-within-the-story format. That's what I did above with the mini-lesson on ancient Greek drama.

4. Are You in a Human-to-Humans Relationship?

In the end, your relationship with listeners is the key to getting any audience to love listening to you. Your in-the-moment performance is the essence of the public speaking situation. What happens on the stage or in a conference room should never be only about the *transfer* of information. It should always be about the *transformation* of people's lives.

You won't always be giving talks on grand themes that change society, of course. But the ways that you influence people's thoughts, emotions, and behavior, even if those ways are small, matter greatly. There's really only one way to make that happen: to get in there and mix it up, connecting with the folks in the seats and not just reading off information to them.

Recently, following a keynote speech I delivered at a national conference, an audience member asked a question along those lines.

"I've always heard that if you're nervous on stage," he began, "it's best to look at the back wall of the auditorium so it looks as if you're speaking to the people in the last row but so that you don't have to make eye contact. Is that a good idea?"

"That's a silly idea," I replied. That got a laugh, though I wasn't trying for one. "Who do you think will be easier for you to convince," I asked the questioner, "the wall, or your audience? The wall won't listen to you, and it definitely can't be positively changed by you."

Then I finished my reply with a comment that might have had this chapter in mind: "And of course, the wall won't love you back."

It's been quite a journey, hasn't it? At the start of this book, we asked the question whether it's possible to learn leadership presence for public speaking. Then we looked at all the evidence that demonstrates that it certainly is possible—and in fact that we see around us every day in the hands of skilled speakers.

I hope that along the way, you've discovered that you are a natural performer. Through spoken performance, you too are able to make yourself memorable. So, you are already on your way to speaking with stage presence!

You now have in your toolbox the practical applications of breathing, voice, and body language to help make that presence evident. You've discovered how to get an audience on board quickly; and how to use stories to create an emotional response. You've learned the essential personal qualities of speaking for leadership, along with powerful ways to command a stage.

Through these pages, you've journeyed through many topics having to do with dynamic speaking performance. They have ranged from brain chemistry to the use of space; from spirituality to psychology; from the production of vocal sound to using emotions to change people's lives. All of it—and everything else this book has tried to convey—is part of the art and science of speaking for leadership.

APPENDIX A

A Master Class in Public Speaking with Winston Churchill

Famed as an orator and leader of wartime Great Britain in World War II, Sir Winston Churchill has much to teach us about the practical aspects of public speaking presence. In fact, few speakers throughout history matched his skill in consciously using speech performance techniques to fascinate listeners.

Can you use his approach to mesmerize the audiences you speak to? Absolutely!

Let's see how the great politician and orator made his speeches into memorable events.

In the second of three volumes that constitute his brilliant biography *The Last Lion,* William Manchester gives us a glimpse of the Churchill method of giving a speech. Although Churchill was well recognized as an author, historian, and speechwriter of distinction, he had a secret side concerning how he went about delivering his speeches in Parliament. It's a lesson all of us who speak professionally should take to heart.

Here is Churchill the master craftsman at work.

Once Churchill had the final version of a speech, he had it typed on pieces of paper measuring around 4″ × 8″. The text was now set in "broken lines to aid his delivery," or what a British cabinet member called "speech form." When he spoke, therefore, using what his fellow politicians thought was notes, Churchill was actually reading the entire speech word for word from those slips of paper. These were speeches with "an illusion of spontaneity and include[d] stage directions ('pause,' 'grope for word,' and 'stammer; correct self'), each . . . a dramatic, vibrant occasion."[1]

Churchill's unique method is a reminder that in speaking for leadership, one must go beyond organizing a speech well and enter the realm of dramatic performance. Think of it as another example of commanding a stage. Whichever way you characterize it, the method goes straight to the heart of achieving dynamism and credibility in an audience's eyes.

Like all great speakers, Churchill grasped the difference between the literary act of writing a speech and the oral performance when that speech is delivered. Every audience (yours too!) needs a speaker with stage presence to make the material come to life. Actually, exactly the same is true for the speaker.

In other words, Churchill was highly focused on performing his content rather than merely delivering it. Why not think along those lines yourself?

In his book, Manchester quotes critic and philosopher William Hazlitt, who said that "'Splendid prose...should be accompanied by vehemence and gesture, a dramatic tone, flashing eyes, and conscious attitude.' That can serve as a description of Churchillian delivery. [This] consummate performer,"[2] as Manchester calls him, can serve as your model of a speaker who perfectly combines vital content with an exciting style of delivery.

How to Use the Power of Silence

Churchill clearly considered nonverbal delivery to be an essential aspect of speaking effectiveness. That included movement, gestures, voice... and even the hesitations he built into his orations!

Perhaps one of the easiest lessons to take away from what I'm calling The Churchill Method is just that: his recognition of the power of silence in speeches. In fact, to see one of Churchill's speeches transcribed as he actually spoke it is to be struck by the fact that it looks more like poetry than prose.

Here is an example from one of his most famous speeches. It is Churchill's first address to the nation as prime minister, delivered over the radio or "wireless" on May 19, 1940. I've included two versions of the speech below. The first is a portion of the speech exactly as written. The second is the same excerpt, but this time showing how Churchill actually spoke the lines of the speech, i.e., including his phrasing and pauses.

I often use this piece as an exercise in group workshops. I ask for a volunteer to read aloud both versions. (I also ask everyone to close their eyes, since we are supposed to be hearing this over the radio.) Afterwards, I ask everyone about any differences they heard in the two versions.

CHURCHILL'S SPEECH AS WRITTEN

"In the air—often at serious odds, often at odds hitherto thought overwhelming—we have been clawing down three or four to one of our enemies; and the relative balance of the British and German Air Forces is now considerably more favorable to us than at the beginning of the battle. In cutting down the German bombers, we are fighting our own battle as well as that of France. My confidence in our ability to fight it out to the finish with the German Air Force has been strengthened by the fierce encounters which have taken place and are taking place. At the same time, our heavy bombers are striking nightly at the tap-root of German mechanized power, and have already inflicted serious damage upon the oil refineries on which the Nazi effort to dominate the world directly depends."

CHURCHILL'S SPEECH AS SPOKEN

"In the air,
often at serious odds,
often at odds hitherto thought overwhelming—
we have been clawing down three or four to one
of our enemies;
and the relative balance of the British and German Air Forces
is now considerably more favorable to us
than at the beginning of the battle.
In cutting down the German bombers,
we are fighting our own battle as well as that of France.
My confidence in our ability to fight it out to the finish

with the German Air Force

has been strengthened by the fierce encounters

which have taken place and are taking place.

At the same time,

our heavy bombers are striking nightly at the tap-root of German
mechanized power,

and have already inflicted serious damage

upon the oil refineries

on which the Nazi effort

to dominate the world directly depends."

Would you like to hear the difference yourself? You could find one of the recorded versions of Churchill from 1940 and listen to the real thing. Or you could speak the speech out loud yourself and record your two versions: once as the "prose" or literary version, then as the "poetry" of the speaking rendition with its built-in pauses.

You may be amazed at what you hear when you listen to the playback. Churchill's phraseology allows all the images to bloom much more vividly in the mind's eye: "clawing down" the enemy planes; the bombs striking the oil refineries, etc. You'll almost certainly *retain* more of what you heard; and throughout, the ideas should impress themselves upon you much more forcefully in the spoken version.

The story being told, the ideas, the vividness of the imagery—in short, the message and meaning of this speech—all come through far more powerfully. And all because of Churchill's system of intentionally breaking up a speech into 'hearable' units.

It's a reminder that for great public speaking, you must care about your performance as much as you do your content.

That's The Churchill Method in action.

15 Easy Ways to Keep Your Voice Healthy

We've seen how speech is created by the activation of the vocal folds, or "cords." They aren't cords, however, but folds of mucous membrane; hence the name.

These folds vibrate, "modulating the flow of air being expelled from the lungs during phonation."[1] Proper breathing habits and the gentle coming together of the vocal folds facilitate a warm, pleasant voice. Poor breathing; "slamming" the folds together; or subjecting them to harsh conditions inside your voice box result in a strained voice. That type of voice is unpleasant to listen to, often hard to hear, and painful for the speaker to produce.

Below are some steps you can take to avoid bad habits or unfavorable conditions that can leave you with vocal strain or discomfort. They are also, generally, practices to help keep your voice healthy.

THE DO'S

1. **Support your breath.** Do you belly-breathe? Diaphragmatic breathing or using your abdominal area is your body's natural breathing mechanism. Two ways of breathing incorrectly are *thoracic breathing* (moving your chest) and *clavicular breathing* (raising your shoulders). Allowing your diaphragm to descend— so that your belly moves outward—gives your lungs room to expand fully. Exhaling with enough air creates a "pillow" to support the sound and helps project and protect the voice.

2. **Hydrate yourself.** It's important that you keep your vocal folds moist. The drier the mucous membranes, the raspier the sound is. Speech anxiety in particular can shut off the flow of saliva you need for a healthy mouth and throat. If you don't want to look like a lizard flicking its tongue out continually as it delivers a speech, keep yourself hydrated. Plain water is best.

3. **Rest your voice. (Avoid strain, pain, or being drained.)** If you're experiencing strain, pain, or a general energy drain, you need to rest your voice. When that isn't possible, work on speaking more succinctly (fewer words = less speaking). And learn to trust silence.

4. **Keep candy, mints, or cough drops handy.** Anything that keeps your saliva glands active is a good idea, as you'll continually bathe your vocal folds in necessary moisture. Green apples are particularly good at getting those saliva glands working!

5. **Drink tea with lemon and honey.** This combination helps soothe your throat. The tea shouldn't be too hot, of course. And avoid this drink just before speaking, as you don't want to coat your throat with honey.

6. **Hum, focusing the sound on the "mask" of your face.** When you're humming properly, your lips should tingle or feel itchy so you want to scratch them! The idea is to get your sound up and out—to center your sound in the front of your face rather than letting it sink down into your throat and chest. The less you force the sound down into your throat, the more effortlessly and comfortably you'll be able to speak.

7. **Warm up your voice.** Start with the humming exercise just mentioned, then open your mouth wide letting the sound emerge as if you were saying "MAAAAH." (I call this the Crocodile Exercise.) Now let the sound slide both ways through the musical scale, from the lowest pitch you can produce without strain to the highest one, then from high to low. Last, find the center of your range in terms of pitch, and "place" the resulting sound about ten feet in front of you. That will make sure you're not swallowing your voice, but getting it out. Go ahead and sing the sound if you like!

8. **Take a shower.** Nothing personal. The warm water and steam will moisten your vocal apparatus and open your throat. You can also try the vocal warm-up described above in the shower while these conditions apply.

THE DON'TS

9. **Avoid dairy.** Milk, chocolate, and other dairy products coat your throat. A coated throat will produce a muffled sound, and will make you want to clear your throat. As I explain in the next tip, that's not a good thing to do.

10. **Try not to clear your throat.** This "slams" the vocal folds together, rather than the gentle action that should accompany phonation. Anything that increases tension in the voice box or abrades the membranes is counter-productive to healthy sound and can actually be damaging. If you feel you have to get rid of an annoying sensation in your throat, swallow to clear the secretions, or drink water to thin them out.

11. **Don't speak louder.** Instead, think of *using more energy*. To "speak louder" means to increase the tension in your vocal folds, and it usually changes the quality of your voice for the worse. To gain more volume, simply take a sufficient breath then increase the breath-energy traveling upward by consciously contracting or pulling in the diaphragm. You'll create a stronger upward thrust of air to project your voice outwards. Make sure you keep your throat open, i.e., not tight. Doing these things will help you improve your projection without strain.

12. **Don't smoke.** Smoking dries up the vocal folds, and as we know they need to stay moist. It's easy to identify a smoker by their voice alone: it's deeper than it once was, raspier and dry sounding.

13. **Avoid alcohol or caffeinated beverages.** These also dry up your throat. Antihistamines do too. And let's face it: if you're depending upon caffeine to give you energy or alcohol to reduce your nerves, you might consider some lifestyle changes.

14. **Don't whisper.** Some speech coaches and medical professionals believe that whispering damages the voice. Others say it doesn't. Whispering is a speaking technique in which the vocal folds don't vibrate, i.e., the sound is produced without the voice box being activated. That's not necessarily good or bad; it's just one of the ways you can produce spoken sound without the benefit of a full voice. If you do whisper, avoid squeezing your vocal folds together too hard. It isn't necessary and can be harmful.

15. **Eliminate slouching or bad posture.** When you slouch, you reduce your breathing capacity while constricting your throat. That points you in the wrong direction from achieving a healthy and pleasant voice. Of course, slouching also looks bad. As a public speaker, you always need to be thinking of the image you're broadcasting.

Notes

Introduction: All the World's a Stage

1 Chris Anderson, "How to Give a Killer Presentation," *Harvard Business Review,* v. 91, issue 6 (June 2013).

2 David Ball, *Theater Tips and Strategies for Jury Trials,* 2d ed. (South Bend, IN: NITA, 1997), ix–x.

Chapter 1: Can You Learn Leadership Presence? . . . *YES!*

1 Amy Cuddy, *Presence* (Boston: Little, Brown and Company, 2015), 26.

2 Theresa Ruth Howard, "Improving stage presence," *Dance Magazine* v. 82, issue 12. (Dec. 2008). http://link.galegroup.com/apps/doc/A190462060/ PPFA?u=mlin_m_minuteman&sid=PPFA&xid=9e0d2fbb.

3 Johann Wolfgang Von Goethe, "Rules for Actors" (1803, 1824), translated by John Oxenford, 86, 83. https://sites.broadviewpress.com/lessons/ DramaAnthology/GoetheRulesForActors/GoetheRulesForActors_ print.html.

4 Kathy Lubar and Belle Linda Halpern, *Leadership Presence* (New York: Gotham, 2003), 1.

5 Lubar and Halpern, 19.

6 James Whittaker, "Master The Art of Stage Presence," October 6, 2015. https://www. microsoft.com/en-us/microsoft-365/blog/2015/10/06/ master-the-art-of-stage-presence-with-james-whittaker/ Italics in original.

7 Sarah Pini, "Alternative Approaches to the Classic Model of Stage Presence in Performing Arts: A Review." https://www.academia.edu/ Documents/in/Presence_ Performing_Arts_.

8 Anderson, op cit.

9 At least to a young acting student. Interestingly, a friend and I made our way that evening through the labyrinthine backstage corridors of the National complex until we found Gielgud and Richardson's dressing rooms. We were able to chat with a completely gracious John Gielgud; but Ralph Richardson was talking to the director in his dressing room, and we didn't want to disturb them.

10 Veronica Kelly, book review of *Stage Presence* by Jane Goodall, in *Performance Paradigm* 5.1 (2009), 115.

11 https://en.oxforddictionaries.com/definition/charisma.

12 Roger Ailes, *You Are the Message* (New York: Doubleday, 1988), 104–105.

13 Ailes, 153.

14 Richard Dowis, *The Lost Art of the Great Speech* (New York: Amacom, 2000), 5.

15 "Number of commercial TV stations in the United States from 1950 to 2017." https://www.statista.com/statistics/189655/number-of -commercial-television-stations-in-the-us-since-1950/.

16 "There are 15,330 U.S. Radio Stations, But How Many Matter?" https://www.hypebot.com/hypebot/2013/10/there-are-15330-us -radio-stations-how-many-of-the-matter-to-you.html.

17 "Number of daily newspapers in the United States from 1970 to 2016." https://www.statista.com/statistics/183408/number-of-us-daily -newspapers-since-1975/.

18 "Unique visitors of newspaper websites." https://www.journalism.org /fact-sheet/newspapers/.

19 "Americans' online news use is closing in on TV news use," September 7, 2017. https://www.pewresearch.org/fact-tank/2017/09/07/americans -online-news-use-vs-tv-news-use/.

Chapter 2: Why You're a Natural Performer

1 Patsy Rodenburg, *The Actor Speaks* (New York: St. Martin's, 2000), 15.

2 L. Balachandra, "Keep Calm and Pitch On: Balancing and Moderating Affect in the Entrepreneur's Pitch," 2015. Manuscript submitted for publication. Quoted in Cuddy, 19.

3 Cuddy, 198.

4 Cicely Berry, *The Actor and the Text* (New York: Applause, 1992), 11.

5 Jim McElhaney, "More Than Just Words: This Is What It Really Means to Talk Like a Lawyer," *ABA Journal*, January 1, 2012.

6 Lubar and Halpern, 234–235.

7 Jana Childers, *Performing the Word: Preaching as Theatre* (Nashville: Abingdon Press, 1998), 20.

8 Richard Ward, *Speaking from the Heart: Preaching with Passion* (Nashville: Abingdon Press, 1992), 77. Quoted in Childers, 48.

9 Rob Weinert-Kendt, "Stage Presence: A spirituality of theater," *America*, May 2, 2011. http://link.galegroup.com/apps/doc/A255971013/ PPFA?u=mlin_m_minuteman&sid=PPFA&xid=7b5cedd0.

10 Childers, 54.

11 Ailes, 92–93.

12 Lubar and Halpern, 253.

Chapter 3: How to Make Yourself Memorable

1 Ailes, 77–78.

2 Even a monologue, which we might think of as the epitome of a one-person delivery of information, is a shared experience. Actors are acutely concerned about what they're "getting back" from the house when they're performing. There is always a palpable sense of the level of energy going back and forth, from the stage to the seats and vice-versa. "How's the house?" is the ever-present question actors coming offstage hear from cast members who haven't made their entrance yet. Reactions are real, even though audience members aren't of course saying anything out loud.

3 Bruce McConachie. *Engaging Audiences* (New York: Palgrave Macmillan, 2008), 1, 7.

4 Dowis, 89.

5 Ailes, 83.

6 Martha Burns, "Dopamine and Learning: What the Brain's Reward Center Can Teach Educators," *Scientific Learning*, September 18, 2012. https://www.scilearn.com/blog dopamine-learning-what-brain%E2%80%99s-reward-center-can-teach-educators.

7 Berry, *Voice and the Actor* (New York: Collier, 1973), 19.

8 Ibid., 77.

Chapter 4: Overcoming Nerves and Speaking with Confidence

1 Dowis, 21.

2 Karen Kangas Dwyer, *Conquer Your Speechfright* (Fort Worth: Harcourt Brace, 1998), 3–12.

3 Gary Genard, *Fearless Speaking* (Arlington, MA: Cedar & Maitland Press, 2014), 217. The numbers are updated here since the publication of this earlier book.

4 Quoted in Mel Gussow, "Henry Higgins Is Real (and Female)," *The New York Times,* January 8, 2001.

5 Rich Karlgaard, "It's Never Too Late to Start a Brilliant Career," *The Wall Street Journal,* May 4–5, 2019, C1.

6 Rita Carter. *The Human Brain Book* (London: DK Publishing, 2014), 64.

7 John Ratey. *A User's Guide to the Brain* (New York: Pantheon, 2001), 232.

8 Daniel Goleman, *Emotional Intelligence* (New York: Bantam, 1995), 297.

9   Carter, 126–127.

10 Caroline Williams. *My Plastic Brain* (Amherst, NY: Prometheus, 2018), 77–78.

11 52 Hofmann and Otto, *Cognitive Behavioral Therapy for Social Anxiety Disorder,* 16, citing a study by L.-G. Lundh and L.-G. Öst, "Recognition bias for critical faces in social phobics," in *Behaviour Research and Therapy,* 34, 787–794 (1996). In the study, subjects with social anxiety disorder or SAD and controls were asked to judge from photographs whether people were critical or accepting in nature. After performing an unrelated task, both groups were given a facial recognition test. People with social anxiety disorder more easily recognized the people they thought had critical faces, while the control subjects had a tendency to recall "accepting" faces. Quoted in Genard, *Fearless Speaking,* 96.

12 Anna LeMind, "Top 10 Most Common Human Fears and Phobias." Learning-Mind.com. https://www.learning-mind.com/top-10-most-common-human-fears-and-phobias/

13 If fear of public speaking is an overriding issue for you, you'll find a complete 12-day course for eliminating your stage fright in my book *Fearless Speaking.* The book is a comprehensive self-guided program with 50 assessment instruments, exercises, visualizations, and approaches for understanding and overcoming speaking fear. You can find the book on The Genard Method's web site at https://www.genardmethod.com/help-with-fear-of-public-speaking-and-stage-fright, or on Amazon at https://www.amazon.com/Fearless-Speaking-Anxiety-Confidence-Change/dp/0979631408/ref=sr_1_3?keywords=fearless+speaking&qid=1570806377&sr=8-3.

14 Kara E. Hannibal and Mark D. Bishop, "Chronic Stress, Cortisol Dysfunction, and Pain: A Psychoneuroendocrine Rationale for Stress Management in Pain Rehabilitation." https://www.ncbi.nlm.nih.gov/pmc/articles/PMC4263906/.

Chapter 5: Breathing for Focus and Power

1   Dennis Lewis. *Free Your Breath, Free Your Life* (Boston: Shambhala, 2004), 98.

2   Ibid., 99, quoting Karlfried Graf von Durckheim.

3   Lubar and Halpern, 31.

4   https://voicefoundation.org/health-science/voice-disorders/anatomy-physiology-of-voice-production/understanding-voice-production/.

5 Childers, 58.

6 Berry, *The Actor and the Text,* 24.

7 Lewis, 135.

8 Berry, op. cit., 27–28.

Chapter 6: Vocal Dynamics: Transforming Your Relationship with Your Audience

1 Berry, *Voice and the Actor,* 76.

2 Kristin Linklater. *Freeing the Natural Voice* (New York: Drama Book Publishers, 1976), 28.

3 Rodenburg, 5.

4 Quoted in Lubar and Halpern, 134.

5 Ailes, 122–124.

6 Berry, *The Actor and the Text,* 101.

7 Peter Brook, Foreword to Berry, *Voice and the Actor,* 1.

8 John Barton. *Playing Shakespeare* (London: Methuen Drama, 1989), 50.

Chapter 7: Body Language: The Art of Physical Expression

1 Joe Navarro, *What Every Body Is Saying* (New York: William Morrow, 2008), 4, quoting Burgoon, 1994, 229–285.

2 Albert Mehrabian, *Silent Messages* (Belmont, CA: Wadsworth, 1981), 75–80.

3 Daniel Goleman, *Emotional Intelligence* (New York: Bantam, 1995), 97.

4 https://en.wikipedia.org/wiki/Jill_Bolte_Taylor.

5 Cuddy, 40.

6 Carmine Gallo. *Talk Like TED* (New York: St. Martin's Griffin, 2014), 90. Quoting Morgan Wright, Chief Crime Fighter, Washington, D.C. Metro Area, in discussion with the author, April 4, 2013.

7 Cuddy, 224.

8 Alex Noppe, "Effects of Stage Presence on Perceptions of Instrumental Performance in Western Classical Music." Unpublished doctoral dissertation. Submitted to the faculty of the Jacobs School of Music in partial fulfillment of the requirements for the degree, Doctor of Music, Indiana University, December 2012, p. 4.

9 Goleman, 96.

10 Cohen Ambrose, "The Stage Presence of the Spiritual Meme," *Theatre Symposium,* v. 21, 2013. Citing Bruce McConachie, *Engaging Audiences: A Cognitive Approach to Spectating in the Theatre* (New York: Palgrave Macmillan, 2008), and Giacomo Rizzolatti and his team of neuroscientists at the University of Parma, Italy (mirror neurons). http://link.galegroup.com/apps/doc/A359332239/PPFA?u=mlin_m_minuteman&sid=PPFA&xid=8d5ceda5.

11 Navarro, 23.

12 Ibid., 22–23.

13 Paul Ekman, *Telling Lies* (New York: W.W. Norton, 1992), 127.

14 Navarro, 165.

Chapter 8: Grab 'Em in Sixty Seconds! — How to Start a Speech

1 Jeff Fleming, "Observational Humor: Seeing What Others Are Thinking," *Professional Speaker,* November 2005, 10.

Chapter 9: Storytelling to Create an Emotional Response

1 Gallo, 144.

2 Op. cit., 145, quoting John Medina, molecular biologist, and author of *Brain Rules* (Seattle: Pear Press; 2d ed., 2014).

3 John J. Ratey, *A User's Guide to the Brain* (New York: Pantheon, 2001), 121.

4 Ibid., 341–346.

5 This is why it's only half-humorous to say, "You can't think and speak at the same time." When you speak to an audience, what you say must have immediate impact. As listeners, we can't get the sense that you're musing about all of it and finding the right next thing to say (some speakers definitely give that impression). You need to be completely in the moment, which in a sense means getting out of your head and into your body, and into the performance space. Some speakers think that if they try to do this, they will lose their grasp of the content of the presentation. But if you know your topic and you've rehearsed sufficiently, that will never happen. You'll retain everything you want to say, while gaining a link to the moment and the audience. That outcome isn't possible unless you're specifically aiming for it to happen.

6 Bruce McConachie. *Engaging Audiences* (New York: Palgrave Macmillan, 2008), 67.

7 Gallo, 51.

8   Andrew Stanton, "The Clues to a Great Story," TED 2012. https://www
    .ted.com/talks/andrew_stanton_the_clues_to_a_great_story#t-99643.

9   Chris Anderson, "How to Give a Killer Presentation."

10 Peter Guber, *Tell to Win: Connect, Persuade, and Triumph with the Hidden
    Power of Stories* (New York: Crown Business, 2011), vii, 9. Quoted in
    Gallo, 66.

11 Ball, 101.

12 Ray Bradbury, *Zen in the Art of Writing* (Santa Barbara, CA: Joshua Odell
    Editions, 1996), 3–4.

Chapter 10: The 7 Essential Qualities of Speaking for Leadership

1   Carmine Gallo, "New Survey: 70% Say Presentation Skills Are Critical for
    Career Success," *Forbes,* September 25, 2014.

2   Boris Groysberg, "The Seven Skills You Need to Thrive in the C-Suite,"
    Harvard Business Review, March 18, 2014.

3   Boris Groysberg and Michael Slind, "Leadership Is a Conversation,"
    Harvard Business Review, June 2012.

4   John Baldoni, *The Leader's Pocket Guide: 101 Indispensable Tools, Tips, and
    Techniques for Any Situation* (New York: Amacom, 2013), 11.

5   "The Value of Centered Leadership: McKinsey Global Survey results,"
    October 2010. http://www.mckinsey.com/global-themes/leadership/
    the-value-of-centered-leadership-mckinsey-global-survey-results.

6   Here, however, we must exempt some movie stars who take almost no
    risks and basically play themselves in film after film. They are really screen
    personalities. You probably know well who they are.

Chapter 11: 5 Powerful Ways to Command a Stage

1   In another words, you mustn't aim for the effect, but to earn a genuine
    emotional response. Here's a time I was guilty of taking the cheap route:
    As part of our studies at the Webber Douglas Academy of Dramatic Art
    in London, we had to take tutorials, or private sessions, with some of the
    teachers. One of the classes was textual study, taught by a very grand and
    elegant elderly lady named Judith Gick. I had prepared a monologue from
    one of Shakespeare's plays, and in her tiny office, she asked me to perform
    it for her. When I finished, she said: "That was excellent second-rate
    acting." She didn't have to explain any further—I knew exactly what she
    was saying. I was going for the emotional payoff, you might say, without
    paying the price of admission. I was acting to dazzle, not to be true to the
    character and the moment in that person's life.

2 http://www.historyplace.com/speeches/washington.htm.

3 A few years ago, I was training a group of 50 salespeople in Chicago for a company that had a young workforce. I was discussing this subject, and I asked the group what they thought happened in 800 B.C. in Western civilization that I was referring to. One of them shouted: "The dinosaurs died out!" To howls of laughter from his colleagues, he smiled shyly and said, "Oh … I guess not."

Appendix A: A Master Class in Public Speaking with Winston Churchill

1 William Manchester, *The Last Lion: Alone 1932–1940* (New York: Delta/ Dell, 1988), 33–34.

2 Ibid., 104.zzz

Appendix B: 15 Easy Ways to Keep Your Voice Healthy

1 https://www.sciencedaily.com/terms/vocal_folds.htm#:~:text=The%20 vocal%20folds%2C%20also%20known,from%20the%20lungs%20 during%20phonation.

Index

Speak at Your Best Professionally!

Also by Dr. Gary Genard

Available as signed paperback editions and ebooks at www.genardmethod.com

A fast-paced guide to more dynamic speeches, meetings, pitches, and presentations. Discover 101 ways to build your confidence and skills for more influential speaking! Learn the approach that has helped CEOs, management teams, entrepreneurs, and professionals worldwide.

Is stage fright or self-consciousness about public speaking holding you back? This book will help you permanently overcome your fears and anxieties about your own performance. Includes 50 hands-on exercises. Named as **"One of 100 Best Confidence Books of All Time."**

We're all virtual now! Do you excel at online meetings, videoconferences, and webinars? Learn how you and your team can speak to influence in the online world. Discover today's new rules for personal and team success!

Cedar &
Maitland
Press

Made in the USA
Middletown, DE
06 March 2023